COMMON CORE
Third Grade

**Daily
Skill Practice**

Grade 3

Carson-Dellosa Publishing, LLC
Greensboro, North Carolina

Credits

Content Editors: Elise Craver, Christine Schwab, Angela Triplett
Proofreader: Karen Seberg

 Visit *carsondellosa.com* for correlations to Common Core, state, national, and Canadian provincial standards.

Carson-Dellosa Publishing, LLC
PO Box 35665
Greensboro, NC 27425 USA
carsondellosa.com

ISBN 978-1-4838-1237-3
01-213141151

Table of Contents

Introduction

Common Core Third Grade 4 Today is a perfect supplement to the third-grade classroom curriculum. Students' skills will grow as they support their knowledge of math, language arts, science, and social studies with a variety of engaging activities.

This book covers 40 weeks of daily practice. Each day will provide students with cross-curricular content practice. During the course of four days, students complete questions and activities in math, language arts, science, and social studies in about 10 minutes. On the fifth day of each week, students complete a writing assessment that corresponds with one of the week's activities.

Various skills and concepts in math and language arts are reinforced throughout the book through activities that align to the Common Core State Standards. The standards covered for each week are noted at the bottom of each week's assessment page. For an overview of the standards covered, please see the Common Core State Standards Alignment Matrix on pages 5 to 8.

Indicates the weekly practice page

Indicates the daily practice problems

Indicates the weekly assessment

Indicates the Common Core State Standards covered in the weekly assessment

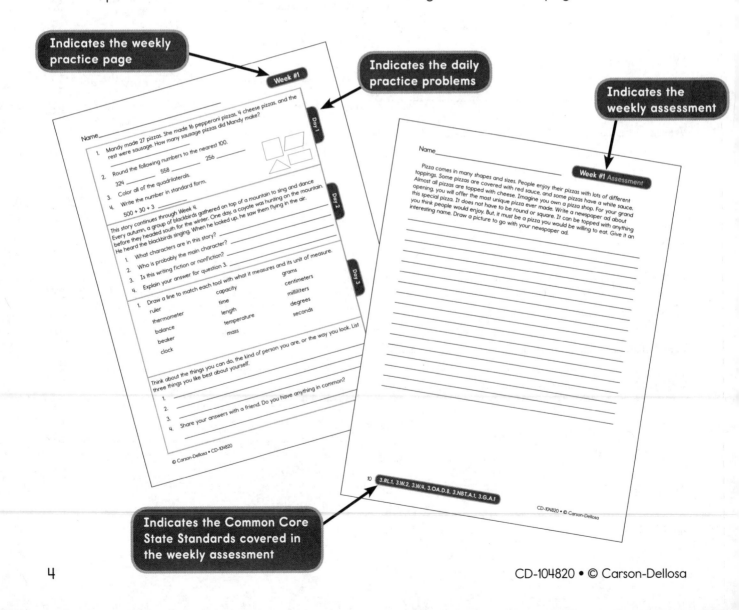

Language Arts

STANDARD	W1	W2	W3	W4	W5	W6	W7	W8	W9	W10	W11	W12	W13	W14	W15	W16	W17	W18	W19	W20
3.RL.1	●	●										●			●	●				
3.RL.2																				
3.RL.3		●	●	●											●					
3.RL.4				●											●	●				
3.RL.5																				
3.RL.6																				
3.RL.7																				
3.RL.9																				
3.RL.10																				
3.RI.1					●	●	●	●		●	●	●		●	●	●		●		
3.RI.2						●														
3.RI.3		●		●																●
3.RI.4			●			●			●									●		
3.RI.5																				
3.RI.6																				
3.RI.7																				
3.RI.8																				
3.RI.9																				
3.RI.10		●			●		●	●		●					●					
3.RF.3		●						●							●					
3.RF.4																				
3.W.1							●		●					●			●			
3.W.2	●		●	●			●	●			●	●	●						●	
3.W.3		●			●	●				●	●				●	●	●	●		●
3.W.4	●	●	●				●						●				●			
3.W.5						●							●						●	
3.W.6					●		●			●										
3.W.7			●				●						●						●	
3.W.8					●									●						
3.W.10																				
3.SL.1																				
3.SL.2																				
3.SL.3																				
3.SL.4												●								
3.SL.5																				
3.SL.6																				
3.L.1					●		●		●		●		●				●		●	
3.L.2					●		●				●		●				●		●	
3.L.3																				
3.L.4								●	●					●				●		
3.L.5																				
3.L.6												●								

W = Week

Language Arts

STANDARD	W21	W22	W23	W24	W25	W26	W27	W28	W29	W30	W31	W32	W33	W34	W35	W36	W37	W38	W39	W40
3.RL.1								●									●			
3.RL.2																	●			
3.RL.3																				
3.RL.4								●												
3.RL.5																				
3.RL.6																				
3.RL.7																				
3.RL.9																				
3.RL.10																				
3.RI.1	●	●	●							●	●	●	●	●	●		●		●	●
3.RI.2		●	●	●	●									●		●				
3.RI.3										●					●				●	
3.RI.4	●					●					●					●				
3.RI.5																				
3.RI.6																				
3.RI.7								●												
3.RI.8																				
3.RI.9																				
3.RI.10										●							●		●	●
3.RF.3	●					●		●				●	●	●		●	●			
3.RF.4																				
3.W.1					●			●							●			●		
3.W.2			●	●		●	●				●	●							●	●
3.W.3	●	●							●	●			●	●	●	●	●			
3.W.4					●		●						●						●	
3.W.5					●				●				●	●						
3.W.6							●										●			
3.W.7			●			●	●				●								●	
3.W.8			●			●	●				●			●				●	●	
3.W.10							●				●						●			
3.SL.1																				
3.SL.2																				
3.SL.3																				
3.SL.4																				
3.SL.5																				
3.SL.6																				
3.L.1							●		●									●		●
3.L.2							●		●									●		●
3.L.3							●		●									●		
3.L.4	●				●	●	●	●	●		●	●	●	●		●	●			
3.L.5																				
3.L.6												●								

W = Week

Common Core State Standards Alignment Matrix

Math

STANDARD	W1	W2	W3	W4	W5	W6	W7	W8	W9	W10	W11	W12	W13	W14	W15	W16	W17	W18	W19	W20
3.OA.A.1													●	●						
3.OA.A.2																				
3.OA.A.3				●				●					●				●	●		●
3.OA.A.4															●	●	●		●	●
3.OA.B.5											●								●	
3.OA.B.6																				
3.OA.C.7											●	●			●	●			●	
3.OA.D.8	●			●	●				●			●			●					
3.OA.D.9			●			●						●						●		
3.NBT.A.1	●				●				●				●							
3.NBT.A.2		●	●	●	●	●	●		●	●	●	●	●	●			●	●	●	●
3.NBT.A.3																	●			
3.NF.A.1																				
3.NF.A.2																				
3.NF.A.3																				
3.MD.A.1				●												●				
3.MD.A.2																				
3.MD.B.3		●					●			●				●						
3.MD.B.4																				
3.MD.C.5																				
3.MD.C.6																				
3.MD.C.7																				
3.MD.D.8																				
3.G.A.1	●						●	●							●					
3.G.A.2					●															

W = Week

Common Core State Standards Alignment Matrix

Math

STANDARD	W21	W22	W23	W24	W25	W26	W27	W28	W29	W30	W31	W32	W33	W34	W35	W36	W37	W38	W39	W40
3.OA.A.1																				
3.OA.A.2																				
3.OA.A.3		●			●	●	●					●							●	
3.OA.A.4	●																			
3.OA.B.5				●	●					●							●			
3.OA.B.6																				
3.OA.C.7																				
3.OA.D.8									●											
3.OA.D.9			●															●	●	
3.NBT.A.1								●								●				●
3.NBT.A.2				●		●		●			●			●		●		●		●
3.NBT.A.3												●			●					
3.NF.A.1			●							●						●				●
3.NF.A.2	●						●													
3.NF.A.3		●		●	●		●	●			●		●		●					
3.MD.A.1														●	●		●			
3.MD.A.2											●									
3.MD.B.3														●						
3.MD.B.4			●			●			●								●			
3.MD.C.5																				
3.MD.C.6												●								
3.MD.C.7													●					●		
3.MD.D.8													●					●	●	●
3.G.A.1																●				
3.G.A.2		●								●										

W = Week

CD-104820 • © Carson-Dellosa

1. Mandy made 27 pizzas. She made 16 pepperoni pizzas, 4 cheese pizzas, and the rest were sausage. How many sausage pizzas did Mandy make?

   _____

2. Round the following numbers to the nearest 100.

   324 _____   558 _____   256 _____

3. Color all of the quadrilaterals.

4. Write the number in standard form.

   500 + 30 + 3 _____

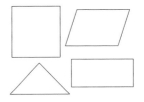

This story continues through Week 4.
Every autumn, a flock of blackbirds gathered on top of a mountain to sing and dance before they headed south for the winter. One day, a coyote was hunting on the mountain. He heard the blackbirds singing. When he looked up, he saw them flying in the air.

1. What characters are in this story? _____

2. Who is probably the main character? _____

3. Is this writing fiction or nonfiction? _____

4. Explain your answer for question 3. _____

1. Draw a line to match each tool with what it measures and its unit of measure.

   ruler   capacity   grams

   thermometer   time   centimeters

   balance   length   milliliters

   beaker   temperature   degrees

   clock   mass   seconds

Think about the things you can do, the kind of person you are, or the way you look. List three things you like best about yourself.

1. _____

2. _____

3. _____

4. Share your answers with a friend. Do you have anything in common?

   _____

Name_____

    Pizza comes in many shapes and sizes. People enjoy their pizzas with lots of different toppings. Some pizzas are covered with red sauce, and some pizzas have a white sauce. Almost all pizzas are topped with cheese. Imagine you own a pizza shop. For your grand opening, you will offer the most unique pizza ever made. Write a newspaper ad about this special pizza. It does not have to be round or square. It can be topped with anything you think people would enjoy. But, it must be a pizza you would be willing to eat. Give it an interesting name. Draw a picture to go with your newspaper ad.

_____

_____

_____

_____

_____

_____

_____

_____

_____

_____

_____

_____

_____

_____

_____

Name_____

1.   88 – 32 = _____

2.   What units would you use to measure the length of a wall?

    A. inches   B. centimeters   C. yards

3.   How many books did Brad, April, and Travis
     read altogether? _____

Books Read over the Summer

This story began on Week 1.

   "How beautifully you fly and dance!" the coyote cried. "Can you teach me to do that? If I could fly, I could be the great king of the coyotes."

   The blackbirds knew the coyote could never fly, but they wanted to have some fun. "We can teach you to fly. Come to the top of the mountain, and we will assist you."

1.   Write the word from the story that is a compound word. _____

2.   What other word could you use instead of **assist** in this story? _____

3.   What can you tell about the character of the blackbirds? _____

4.   Would you say the coyote is proud or humble? _____
     Underline the sentence that supports your answer.

When most people in the United States measure, they use the **customary system**. Length is measured in inches and feet. Weight is measured in pounds. Capacity uses cups, pints, and gallons. Most other people in the world use the **metric system**. Every measurement is based on a unit of ten. A meter measures length. There are 100 centimeters in a meter. A liter measures capacity. There are 100 centiliters in a liter. Scientists all over the world, even in the United States, work with the metric system.

1.   Why might all scientists use the metric system?

     _____

There are many workers who help make a community a great place to live. Some of these workers are volunteers who donate their time but do not receive pay for their work. Think about how you can make your community a better place.

1.   Make a list of jobs that you can do to help your community.

     _____

     _____

     _____

2.   Name a place you could volunteer in your community.

     _____

Imagine that your little brother or best friend just got his first bicycle. Try to remember what it was like when you rode a big bike for the first time. It was hard! It was also a lot of fun. Help your brother or friend learn how to ride. Teach him about safety. Write an essay telling him what to do, step by step. Remember to include safety tips.

_____

_____

_____

_____

_____

_____

_____

_____

_____

_____

_____

_____

_____

_____

_____

_____

_____

_____

_____

_____

_____

_____

_____

_____

_____

3.RL.1, 3.RL.3, 3.RI.3, 3.RI.10, 3.RF.3, 3.W.3, 3.W.4, 3.NBT.A.2, 3.MD.B.3

1. 748 − 459 = _____

2. Write the following number in expanded form.

   548 _____

3. Complete the table.

Subtract 11	
23	12
78	
34	

This story began on Week 1.
When the coyote got to the mountaintop, the birds told him to sit down. Then, each bird pulled a feather from his shiny black suit. "This will hurt," said the birds. "But, this is the only way you will be able to fly."

1. What sound does the **ui** in **suit** make: **oo** as in **boot** or **u** as in **cup**? _____

2. What is each bird's "shiny black suit"? _____

3. Would you say the blackbirds are mean or funny? Explain. _____

   _____

4. Do you think the coyote will let the blackbirds hurt him? Explain. _____

   _____

Match each word from the word bank to the correct definition.

balance	graduated cylinder	mass	volume

1. _____ a tool used to measure the volume of a liquid

2. _____ the amount of matter in an object

3. _____ the amount of space that matter occupies

4. _____ a tool used to calculate the mass of an object

Mischa and her friends were playing baseball in an empty lot. Mischa was at bat. She swung hard and the ball sailed across the lot and smashed through a neighbor's window. Mischa knew the neighbor would be really angry. The other kids scattered.

1. What should Mischa do next?

   _____

2. Is it always easy to do the right thing? Explain.

   _____

   _____

Imagine that you are given a 15-gallon aquarium for your birthday. Use the Internet, books, or magazines to research the kind of fish to buy. Find out what kind of water they need. Learn about the food they eat. Think about decorations and plants. There is a lot to learn about owning an aquarium! Write a report to tell how you will set up your aquarium. Use facts and definitions to explain.

_____

_____

_____

_____

_____

_____

_____

_____

_____

_____

_____

_____

_____

_____

_____

_____

_____

_____

_____

_____

_____

_____

_____

1. Pablo wants to play flag football with 9 of his friends. Each player needs 2 flags. How many flags are needed so that all 9 friends and Pablo can play flag football together? _____

2. Draw hands on the clock to show 9:05.

3. 768 – 479 = _____

Day 1

This story began on Week 1.
The birds all stuck feathers into the coyote's legs and tail. The feathers jabbed terribly, but the coyote said nothing. He sat very still until the birds had finished. All the while, he was thinking of what a great king he would be.

1. What word from the story means "poked with a sharp point"? _____

2. Did the coyote let the blackbirds hurt him? Explain. _____

3. Do you think the feathers will make the coyote king? Explain. _____

    _____

4. Would you say the coyote is brave or foolish? _____

Day 2

---

1. Planning and conducting experiments are two important process skills. The steps must be done in a certain order for the experiment to work. Below is an experiment about digestion. Write numbers **1** through **5** to show the correct order of steps for the experiment.

    _____ Count to 30 slowly without chewing the cracker.

    _____ Put the cracker in your mouth.

    _____ Use a mirror to see what the cracker looks like in your mouth.

    _____ Draw a picture of the cracker after counting to 30.

    _____ Get a cracker. Draw a picture of it.

Day 3

Many laws are different from community to community. In some places, people must wear helmets when riding bikes. In other places, young people have to be home by a certain hour at night. Think about your own community.

1. What is a law in your community? _____

2. Do you agree or disagree with this law? Why? _____

    _____

Day 4

Is there a law that you think your community should have but does not? Write a letter to the editor of your local newspaper. Explain your idea for this law and why you think it is important. Use facts, definitions, and details to explain.

_____

_____

_____

_____

_____

_____

_____

_____

_____

_____

_____

_____

_____

_____

_____

_____

_____

_____

_____

_____

_____

_____

_____

3.RL.3, 3.RL.4, 3.RI.3, 3.W.2, 3.OA.A.3, 3.OA.D.8, 3.NBT.A.2, 3.MD.A.1

1. Write the fraction that is represented by this rectangle.

   _____

2. Round each number to the nearest 10. Then, add.

   41 + 129 is about _____ .

3. In one hour, Miranda hiked 342 feet. In another two hours, Miranda hiked 512 feet. If the mountain is 1,000 feet high, how many more feet does Miranda have to hike? _____

Rewrite the story title with the correct capital letters.

1. "rudy's rowdy robots" _____

Write **a** if the word begins with a consonant sound. Write **an** if the word begins with a vowel sound.

2. _____ lilac   _____ Indian paintbrush

Write the missing commas in the sentence.

3. Does Ivan live in Illinois Idaho or Iowa?

Read each plural noun. Write the matching singular noun.

4. children _____   tomatoes _____

Data is a collection of facts from which conclusions can be drawn. Data can be recorded in graphs and charts. Scientists interpret data by studying scientific measurements and observations. They use their conclusions about data to respond to a question. For example, when we want to know what the weather will be for the day, we listen to meteorologists. They use data they have collected and interpreted to make an accurate forecast.

1. Why might a scientist need to interpret data? _____

   _____

1. Think about the following situations. Choose one and write a responsible solution to the problem. Share your solution with a friend.

   A. A classmate asks to borrow lunch money from you.

   B. A classmate is bullying your friend on the playground.

   _____

   _____

   _____

Hiking up a mountain is good exercise. It is also a great way to see nature. Think about a hike you have gone on. Or, maybe you have taken a long walk in a park. What do you remember? What did you see that was special? How did you feel after the hike? Write an essay to tell about your hike. Include details to describe thoughts, feelings, or actions. Then, type it on a computer. Read your essay to a friend.

_____

_____

_____

_____

_____

_____

_____

_____

_____

_____

_____

_____

_____

_____

_____

_____

_____

_____

_____

_____

_____

_____

_____

_____

3.RI.1, 3.RI.10, 3.W.3, 3.W.6, 3.W.8, 3.L.1, 3.L.2, 3.OA.D.8, 3.NBT.A.1, 3.NBT.A.2, 3.G.A.2

1. 476 – 267 = _____

2. Write **<**, **>**, or **=** to make each statement true.

   164 ◯ 146   578 ◯ 587   902 ◯ 902

3. Count by 100s.

   594, 694, _____ , 894, _____

4. Complete the number pattern.

   66, 69, 72, _____, _____, _____

The Navajo tribes lived in the Southwestern United States. Their homes, called **hogans**, were made of wood and mud and were built in different shapes. Some hogans were shaped like domes. Others were shaped like hexagons or octagons.

1. Which word in this paragraph is a compound word? _____

2. What is a **hogan**? _____

3. Underline the sentence that is the main idea of this paragraph.

4. List one detail that supports the main idea. _____

Write the name of the step in the scientific method being described.

1. Plan and conduct an investigation or activity. _____

2. Predict what the results of the investigation will be. _____

3. Prepare and share a report that shows the data. _____

4. Draw a conclusion from the results of the investigation. _____

Located in New York Harbor, Ellis Island was once used as the entrance to the United States. It was nicknamed the "Golden Door." **Immigrants**, or people from other countries, came to Ellis Island by boat. When the boats arrived at the island, immigration officers checked immigrants' health records and papers from their home countries. Many of them passed the inspection and were allowed to enter the United States to live and work.

1. What is Ellis Island? _____

2. Who are **immigrants**? _____

3. What was Ellis Island nicknamed? _____

Name_____

When Helen Keller was born she could see, hear, and make sounds. She started talking when she was six months old. Then, she became sick when she was two years old. She lost her sight, speech, and hearing. Later, Helen Keller had a long and happy life. But, at first, she was very unhappy. Write a story about how your life would change if you were suddenly unable to see, hear, and speak. Include details to describe feelings, thoughts, or actions. Give your story a happy ending. Show your story to your teacher. Make changes if needed.

_____

_____

_____

_____

_____

_____

_____

_____

_____

_____

_____

_____

_____

_____

_____

_____

_____

_____

_____

_____

_____

_____

3.RI.1, 3.RI.2, 3.RI.4, 3.W.3, 3.W.5, 3.OA.D.9, 3.NBT.A.2

Day 1

1. 254 + 347 = _____

2. How many more students go to bed at 9:00 than at 8:00? _____

3. Write the name of the shape that has no sides and no vertices.

   _____

Third Graders' Bedtimes	
8:00	◇ ◇
8:30	◇
9:00	◇ ◇ ◇ ◇

◇ = 4 students

Day 2

Correct the capitalization errors.

1. alex goes to soccer practice on tuesdays and thursdays.

Circle the correct verb.

2. Isabella (drink, drinks) milk with her dinner.

Add an apostrophe where it is needed.

3. The trees leaves were thick and green.

Look at the picture. Circle the correct plural noun.

4. monkeys   monkies

Day 3

Jane Goodall liked chimpanzees. She went to Africa to learn about them. She spent many years living in a tent in the jungle to watch them. She took careful notes about what she saw. Goodall also photographed and filmed the animals in their natural habitats. She found out many new facts about the chimpanzees and the skills they had. Goodall wrote books and gave talks about her discoveries.

1. What were two characteristics that made Goodall a good scientist? Explain.

   _____

   _____

Day 4

The **Constitution of the United States** is a set of laws and rules that guide how the US government is run. The Constitution explains the jobs and powers of each part of the federal government and states the basic rights of US citizens. The Constitution was designed to be flexible throughout the years as the needs of the citizens changed.

Read each sentence. Write **T** if it is true. Write **F** if it is false.

1. _____ The Constitution cannot be changed.

2. _____ The Constitution explains the jobs of the federal government.

3. _____ The Constitution guides how the government should be run.

Jane Goodall visited the Gombe Stream Game Reserve in Tanzania, Africa, for the first time in 1960. She set out to find wild chimpanzees, watch them, and write about them. This was a hard job, but she loved her work. Use the Internet, books, or magazines to find more information on Jane Goodall's work with chimpanzees. Write about what you learn. End with your opinion of whether you would like to do her job. Give reasons to support your opinion.

_____

_____

_____

_____

_____

_____

_____

_____

_____

_____

_____

_____

_____

_____

_____

_____

_____

_____

_____

_____

_____

_____

_____

1. Melissa placed 4 pictures on each of the 5 shelves in her bedroom. How many pictures did Melissa place on the shelves in all?

    _____

2. What does the number 8 stand for in the number 687?

    _____

3. Color all of the shapes that have 4 vertices.

Wolves, the wild relatives of dogs, live in family groups. Scientists have found that wolves communicate, or talk, to each other with howls, noises, and movements. The wolves use their voices and their bodies to tell each other important information.

1. Does **howls** rhyme with **owls** or **bowls**? _____

2. What other word for **talk** is used in this paragraph? _____

3. Does the **mu** in **communicate** sound more like **mew** or **moo**? _____

4. What do wolves use to communicate? _____

---

1. What are atoms?

    _____

    _____

Identify the state of matter in each picture.

2. _____   3. _____   4. _____

Christopher Columbus wanted to find a new way to reach Asia from Europe. In 1492, Columbus set sail with about 90 men. They sailed on the *Santa Maria*, *Pinta*, and *Niña*. After three long months, they finally landed on an island in the Caribbean Sea. After exploring the nearby islands, Columbus returned to Spain where he became a hero. Columbus sailed back three more times to the "New World," which he still believed to be Asia.

1. What were the names of Columbus's ships?

    _____

2. What did Columbus want to do? _____

3. Why do you think Columbus was considered a hero in Spain?

    _____

Name_____

Christopher Columbus thought that finding a new trade route to Asia would be safer and bring riches to the Europeans. However, voyages and explorations were expensive. Columbus had to convince Queen Isabella of Spain to give him money for his trips. Explain how you would convince the queen to fund your trip if you were Christopher Columbus. Use facts, definitions, and details in your explanation.

_____

_____

_____

_____

_____

_____

_____

_____

_____

_____

_____

_____

_____

_____

_____

_____

_____

_____

_____

_____

_____

_____

3.RI.1, 3.RI.10, 3.RF.3, 3.W.2, 3.L.4, 3.OA.A.3, 3.G.A.1

1. The movie theater has 500 seats. Ms. Avery's class takes 33 seats, and Ms. Hamilton's class takes 27 seats. How many seats are left?
   _____

2. Yolanda has $2.16. Ruby gives Yolanda 3 dimes and 4 pennies. How much money does Yolanda have now? _____

3. 444 + 279 = _____

4. Round each number to the nearest 10. Then, add.

   491 + 203 is about _____ .

Day 1

Rewrite the book title with the correct capital letters.

1. *the biography of helen keller* _____

Circle the helping verb in the sentence. Underline the main verb.

2. Someday, I will teach my dog to fetch.

Write **your** or **you're** to correctly complete the sentence.

3. Please bring _____ sleeping bag.

Day 2

Choose a word from the word bank to complete each sentence.

friction	inertia	lubricant	speed

1. People often slide on ice because there is much less _____ to stop or slow the motion.

2. A car engine needs _____ to prevent friction between the parts.

3. An object stays in motion or at rest unless another force acts on it because of _____ .

4. The _____ of an object is measured by how fast and how far it moves.

Day 3

Read the passage, Then, complete the graphic organizer.

Orville and Wilbur Wright loved the idea of flying. They tested kites and gliders. They made over 700 glider flights at Kitty Hawk in North Carolina. They soon put a small engine on an airplane. On December 17, 1903, they took the first motor-powered flight.

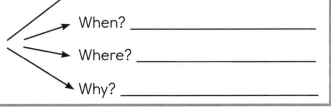

Who? _____

What? _____

When? _____

Where? _____

Why? _____

Day 4

Imagine your parents are taking you and a friend to a movie on Sunday. What movie do you want to see? Why? Your friend wants to see a different movie. What can you tell your friend about your choice to change her mind? Write an essay. Describe the movie you want to see. Give reasons to support your opinion.

_____

_____

_____

_____

_____

_____

_____

_____

_____

_____

_____

_____

_____

_____

_____

_____

_____

_____

_____

_____

_____

_____

_____

3.RI.4, 3.W.1, 3.L.1, 3.L.4, 3.OA.D.8, 3.NBT.A.1, 3.NBT.A.2

1. How many more cars were parked on Wednesday than on Tuesday? _____

2. Add or subtract mentally.

   651 + 100 = _____   495 – 10 = _____

3. 417 – 78 = _____

Cars Parked on Ave. D	
Mon.	🚗 🚗
Tues.	🚗 🚗
Wed.	🚗 🚗 🚗 🚗 🚗

🚗 = 6 cars

Day 1

Japan has a holiday the whole family can enjoy. April is the month for the Cherry Blossom Festival. Cherry trees have flowers for only one week. That week, everyone goes to look at the trees. Entire families go to the park together and stay all day. They take a picnic lunch in a box called an **obentou**. At the park, they eat lunch under the cherry trees. They sing songs and tell stories.

1. What country is this passage talking about? _____

2. What time of year is this passage about? _____

3. Will people celebrate the Cherry Blossom Festival inside or outside? _____
   Why? _____

4. What holidays does your family celebrate? _____

Day 2

What kind of simple machine is each object? Write the name of the machine.

1. scissors _____   2. slide _____

3. fork_____   4. window blinds_____

5. drill _____   6. fishing rod reel _____

7. doorstop _____   8. spring clothespin _____

Day 3

The powers of the federal government are divided into three branches. The **executive** branch carries out the laws. The **legislative** branch makes the laws. The **judicial** branch studies and makes decisions based on the laws.

1. Write **executive**, **judicial**, or **legislative** under the correct picture.

_____   _____   _____

Day 4

Imagine that you awaken one morning and your body has changed. You and your dog have shrunk. You are both suddenly the size of mice. Think about the kind of day you will have together. Write about it. Include details to describe thoughts, feelings, or actions. Read your story to a friend. Make changes if needed. Then, type it on a computer.

_____

_____

_____

_____

_____

_____

_____

_____

_____

_____

_____

_____

_____

_____

_____

_____

_____

_____

_____

_____

_____

_____

1. Which equation is the same as 3 × 2 = 6?

   A. 2 × 3 = 6   B. 6 × 3 = 18

   C. 3 × 6 = 18   D. 6 × 2 = 12

2. 301 – 89 = _____

3. 1 × 8 = _____   5 × 2 = _____   9 × 2 = _____

Correct the capitalization errors.

1. have you ever seen a painting of a huge flower?

Circle the correct adjective.

2. The summer solstice is the (longer, longest) day of the year.

Add the missing apostrophes. Then, write the two words that make up each contraction.

3. isnt _____   shouldnt _____

Read each singular noun. Write the matching plural noun.

4. woman _____   potato _____

1. Describe how a rainbow forms in the sky. Explain your answer to a classmate.

   _____

   _____

   _____

   _____

Read the want ad.

1. How old must a person be to run for president? _____

2. The job of president lasts for a term of _____ years.

3. What is the president's salary per year? _____

Classified
Wanted: President of the United States. Must be at least 35 years old, a natural-born citizen of the US, and have lived in the US for at least 14 years. Job lasts four years. Salary is about $400,000 per year. Experience in politics preferred.

The rain has slowed. The sun peeks through dark clouds. Suddenly, a rainbow appears. It is a huge, beautiful rainbow that begins right where you are standing. Imagine that you can walk over the rainbow like it is a bridge. Where do you think it might take you? Or, where would you like it to take you? Write an essay to answer one of the questions. Include details to describe thoughts, feelings, or actions.

_____

_____

_____

_____

_____

_____

_____

_____

_____

_____

_____

_____

_____

_____

_____

_____

_____

_____

_____

_____

_____

_____

_____

_____

3.RI.1, 3.W.2, 3.W.3, 3.SL.4, 3.L.1, 3.L.2, 3.OA.B.5, 3.OA.C.7, 3.NBT.A.2

1. $1 \times 0 =$ _____ $4 \times 0 =$ _____ $2 \times 2 =$ _____

2. $500 - 250 =$ _____

3. Joey is running a 26-mile marathon. Joey takes a break after 4 miles. He then runs 8 miles more before taking a second break. How many miles does Joey have left to run? _____

4. Write the missing numbers to complete the pattern.

    56, 54, 52, _____ , _____ , _____

March 15, 1405
Dear Father,
   I miss you and the family, but I am happy to be living here and serving Sir Stephen. Castle life is exciting, and I am learning the skills and behavior expected of a knight.

1. Is this story about a knight or a knight in training? _____

2. Is this kind of writing a poem or a letter? _____

3. To whom is the author writing? _____

4. Predict whether the rest of this letter will include details about a job the author finds interesting or boring. _____

1. Which are examples of thermal energy? Circle them.

    lightning   electricity   snowstorm

    wind   burning candle   cooking food

    sun   lemonade   fireworks

2. What is heat?

    _____

    _____

A newly elected president cannot start his job until he takes the oath of office at his inauguration. The president's term begins at noon on January 20 every four years. This oath was written by the Founding Fathers of the United States:
   I do solemnly swear that I will faithfully execute the office of the President of the United States, and will to the best of my ability, preserve, protect, and defend the Constitution of the United States.

1. At what event does the president take his oath of office? _____

2. When? _____

3. Who wrote the presidential oath? _____

Imagine that you have to write a new oath for the president of the United States to take on Inauguration Day. Write the oath based on what you think is important for the president to promise.

_____

_____

_____

_____

_____

_____

_____

_____

_____

_____

_____

_____

_____

_____

_____

_____

_____

_____

_____

_____

_____

_____

_____

_____

1. Jermaine bought 4 boxes of popcorn. Each box has 8 bags of popcorn. How many bags of popcorn does he have?

    _____

2. Round each number to the nearest 10. Then, add.

    34 + 81 is about _____ .

3. Write the multiplication sentence shown by the picture. _____

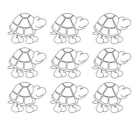

Correct the capitalization errors.

1. mrs. hannah chadwick
    854 pine street
    garnet, montana 59770

Write the correct past-tense form of the irregular verb.

2. They _____ (eat) some little bugs.

Add quotation marks around what a person said.

3. Tony said, I like dogs to.

4. If **to** is used incorrectly in question 3, cross it out and write the correct word above it.

What four kinds of energy can electricity make? Write the name of a device that is an example of each.

1. _____

2. _____

3. _____

4. _____

1. Native American Indians use pictures to tell stories. Look at the picture. Write the story that you think the pictures are trying to tell.

    _____

    _____

    _____

    _____

    _____

People have been popping popcorn for many years. About 500 years ago, young Aztec Indian women danced a popcorn dance. The corn was strung and placed on their heads. Use the Internet, books, and magazines to find out other facts about the history of popcorn. Show the report to your teacher. Make changes if needed.

_____

_____

_____

_____

_____

_____

_____

_____

_____

_____

_____

_____

_____

_____

_____

_____

_____

_____

_____

_____

_____

_____

_____

_____

1. 504 + 298 = _____

2. What was the weather mostly like last week? _____

3. Which addition sentence is the same as 6 × 3?

   A. 6 + 6   B. 3 + 3 + 3 + 3 + 3 + 3

   C. 6 + 6 + 6   D. 3 + 3 + 3

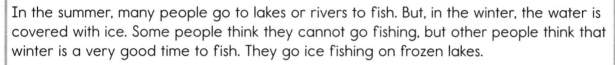

Weather Last Week

In the summer, many people go to lakes or rivers to fish. But, in the winter, the water is covered with ice. Some people think they cannot go fishing, but other people think that winter is a very good time to fish. They go ice fishing on frozen lakes.

1. What time of year do most people go fishing?   A. summer   B. winter

2. What other time of year can people go fishing? _____

3. Where would people fish in winter? _____

4. Write a title for this passage. _____

   _____

Choose a word from the word bank to complete each sentence.

attract	compass	north	poles	repel

1. A _____ is a device that has a magnetized needle.

2. The needle in a compass always points _____.

3. The unlike ends of the magnet _____ each other.

4. The like ends of the magnet _____ each other.

5. The ends of magnets are called _____.

In the early 1970s, Martin Cooper led a team that designed the first practical cell phone. It was 9 inches (22.9 centimeters) long and weighed 2.5 pounds (1.1 km)! It took many years for the United States to develop cellular networks so that people could use their cell phones anywhere in the country. Today, cell phones look much different and can do many more things than the original cell phones.

1. Name one way the cell phone has changed over the years.

   _____

2. How do you think the invention of the cell phone has helped change people's lives? _____

   _____

    Fishing is a good sport to do in the summer. Ice-skating is a good sport to do in the winter. Many people hike in the spring or autumn. Hiking is fun at almost any time of year. What is a sport you enjoy more than any other? When do you do it? What do you like best about it? Write an essay. Give reasons to support your opinions.

_____

_____

_____

_____

_____

_____

_____

_____

_____

_____

_____

_____

_____

_____

_____

_____

_____

_____

_____

_____

_____

_____

3.RI.1, 3.W.1, 3.W.8, 3.L.4, 3.OA.A.1, 3.NBT.A.2, 3.MD.B.3

Day 1

1. _____ × 5 = 35   8 × _____ = 32   3 × 9 = _____

2. Color the quadrilateral.

3. Quinn earns $5 every hour she babysits. Quinn babysits for 6 hours. Then, she goes out for dinner and spends $14. How much money does she have left? _____

4. 4 × 4 = _____   1 × 9 = _____   6 × 3 = _____

Day 2

James is homeless. His orange fur is matted, and his white paws are gray with mud. James is scared of people. He has found a house where a bowl of tuna fish sits on the step every morning.

1. Which word has a suffix that means **without**? _____

2. Is matted fur tangled or fluffy? _____

3. What is James's problem? _____

4. How is James's problem solved? _____

   _____

Day 3

What does it mean to be alive? Living things come in all shapes, sizes, and colors. You can easily see some living things, such as birds, trees, and people. Other living things, such as mold spores and bacteria, are too small to see without a microscope. All living things have several things in common. For example, they are all made of small units called cells. The cells of living things need energy to work, grow, and repair themselves. All living things also need to create new cells as they grow and develop. Nonliving things, such as rocks and trucks, do not grow or develop.

1. What are the small units that make up all living things? _____

2. Cells need _____ to work, grow, and repair themselves.

Day 4

Without fishing and hunting for game, the early **natives** would have starved. The land was rocky and not good for farming. The early Native Americans played games to practice the skills they needed for hunting. The men took turns throwing spears or sticks into a hoop on the ground to improve their accuracy. When hunting became poor, they lived on dried meat and fish.

1. What does **native** mean? _____

2. What did the Native Americans do to practice hunting skills?

   _____

3. What did they eat when there were no animals to hunt?

   _____

All living things are made up of cells. Using the Internet or books, find out more about cells and how they work. Then, try to imagine what would happen if cells could talk. What would they say? Write about a conversation between a cell from your nose and a cell from a dog's nose.

_____

_____

_____

_____

_____

_____

_____

_____

_____

_____

_____

_____

_____

_____

_____

_____

_____

_____

_____

_____

_____

_____

_____

3.RL.1, 3.RL.4, 3.RI.1, 3.RI.10, 3.RF.3, 3.W.3, 3.OA.A.4, 3.OA.C.7, 3.OA.D.8, 3.G.A.1

1. 12 ÷ _____ = 3 _____ ÷ 5 = 3 21 ÷ 3 = _____

2. What time is shown on the clock? _____

3. 4 × 7 = _____

9 × 7 = _____

5 × 8 = _____

Day 1

Evan loves to read books about insects. His class is in the library. He looks in the area where the insect books are usually found. None are there. One of the classes has checked out all of the insect books for reports. He walks to the librarian.

1. Circle the words that can be used instead of **usually**.

   normally   commonly   strangely

2. Why are there no books about insects in the library? _____

3. How do you think Evan feels when he discovers all of the insect books are missing: frustrated or uncaring? _____

4. Predict what will happen next. _____

Day 2

What hereditary traits do these animals have that help them survive in their environments?

1. snakes _____

   _____

2. polar bears _____

   _____

3. camels _____

   _____

Day 3

NASA built a spacecraft called *Apollo 11*. They launched it on July 16, 1969, with three astronauts on board. Four days later, *Apollo 11* reached the moon. On July 20, Neil Armstrong and Buzz Aldrin were the first people to walk on the moon. They took pictures and collected moon rocks and soil samples. When they returned safely to Earth, a huge parade was held for them.

1. What was the name of the spacecraft? _____

2. Who walked on the moon? _____

3. What did the two men do on the moon? _____

   _____

Day 4

Would you have wanted to be one of the first people to walk on the moon? How do you think the men felt as they were heading to the moon for the first time? How would you feel? What do you think they saw when they were in the spacecraft? Write a narrative about what it would be like to travel to and land on the moon. Include details to describe thoughts, feelings, and actions.

_____
_____
_____
_____
_____
_____
_____
_____
_____
_____
_____
_____
_____
_____
_____
_____
_____
_____
_____
_____
_____
_____
_____
_____

3.RL.1, 3.RL.3, 3.RL.4, 3.RI.1, 3.W.3, 3.OA.A.4, 3.OA.C.7, 3.MD.A.1

1. 50 × 3 = _____   60 × 4 = _____   50 × 4 = _____

2. There are 8 girls in Katie's Girl Scout troop. Each girl decorated 3 gingerbread men. How many gingerbread men did the girls decorate altogether?

   _____

3. 436 + 296 = _____

4. 48 ÷ _____ = 8   _____ ÷ 8 = 7   63 ÷ 9 = _____

Correct the capitalization errors.

1. lake superior is the largest lake in the united states.

Circle **S** if the words form a complete sentence. Circle **F** if the words form a fragment.

2. Into the alligator's pond.   S   F

Put the correct mark (**.** **!** **?**) at the end of the sentence.

3. I want to fly my kite ___

Read each sentence. Write **T** if it is true. Write **F** if it is false.

1. _____ Photosynthesis is the process by which plants make their own food.
2. _____ Chlorophyll is the energy source that helps plants make food.
3. _____ Water and carbon dioxide join together inside the leaves.
4. _____ Sugar is the food plants make.
5. _____ Plants give off carbon dioxide as waste.

Rewrite any false statements to make them true.

_____

_____

People who live north or south of the equator have a summer of long days and a winter of short days. People who live at the equator have days and nights of equal length all year long. The **equator** divides the planet in half. The North Pole is located at the very top of the Northern Hemisphere and the South Pole is located at the very bottom of the Southern Hemisphere. There may be 24 hours of either sunlight or darkness at certain times of the year at the poles.

Read each sentence. Write **T** if it is true. Write **F** if it is false.

1. _____ The equator divides the planet into Eastern and Western Hemispheres.
2. _____ People living at the equator have equal lengths of days and nights.
3. _____ The poles can have long periods of either sunlight or darkness.

Find someone who is a member of the Girl Scouts, Boy Scouts, 4-H, or another club for kids. Interview him. Ask about the purpose of the group. Find out what he does at the meetings. Get as much information as you can. Take notes. Then, write an essay about the group. Conclude by stating whether you would like to join the group. Give reasons to support your opinion.

_____

_____

_____

_____

_____

_____

_____

_____

_____

_____

_____

_____

_____

_____

_____

_____

_____

_____

_____

_____

_____

_____

_____

1. Hugo lifted a total of 72 pounds in 9 attempts. Hugo lifted the same number of pounds in each attempt. How many pounds did he lift in each attempt? _____

2. 848 – 399 = _____

3. Complete the table.

Multiply by 7	
1	7
2	
3	
4	
5	

Day 1

Laura Ingalls Wilder wrote eight books about growing up in Wisconsin, Kansas, Minnesota, and South Dakota in the 1800s. She and her family faced many hardships.

1. Who is this passage about? _____

2. What is Laura Ingalls Wilder known for? _____

3. What word in this paragraph is a synonym for the word **problems**?

   _____

4. What hardships do you think Laura and her family faced? _____

   _____

Day 2

Use the words from the word bank to tell how different animals adapt to winter.

adapt	arctic hare	bear	goose	hibernate	migrate

1. Some animals _____ to places that have warm weather in the winter. One such animal is the _____ .

2. Some animals _____ to the cold weather by eating different foods or having body parts that change. The _____ is one of these animals.

3. Another group of animals _____ and sleep through the winter. A _____ does this.

Day 3

---

1. Draw a blue X on the North Pole.

2. Draw a red X on the South Pole.

3. Color North America yellow.

4. The dotted line is called the _____ .

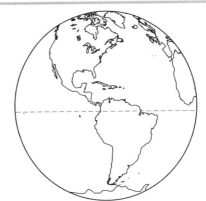

Day 4

Laura Ingalls Wilder wrote stories about the life and travels of a pioneer girl. Much of what she wrote came from her own life. It was not easy living in those days. There were no hospitals nearby in 1867, so Laura was born at home in a log cabin. Laura met some hardships in her life. Her family moved many times. Because they moved so often, Laura and her sisters went to school when they could. But, often they could not go to school and had to teach each other.

Has your family ever had to pack up and move? What hardships did this cause you or your family? If you have never moved, describe what you like and dislike about living in the same place your whole life. Include details to describe thoughts, feelings, or actions.

_____

_____

_____

_____

_____

_____

_____

_____

_____

_____

_____

_____

_____

_____

_____

_____

_____

_____

_____

_____

_____

Name_____

Day 1

1. Samantha is planting tomatoes. She plants 5 rows of 4 tomato seedlings. How many tomato seedlings does Samantha plant altogether? _____

2. Lake Erie is 241 miles long. Lake Ontario is 193 miles long. How many miles long are Lake Erie and Lake Ontario altogether? _____

3. Show two ways to solve this problem. $8 \times 2 \times 5$

4. $24 \div 8 =$ _____ $30 \div 6 =$ _____ $18 \div 2 =$ _____

Day 2

Correct the capitalization errors.

1. aunt irene moved to culver city, california, in april.

Circle the correct word.

2. Alfonso (sets, sits) in the front seat with his father.

Add a comma where it is needed.

3. Well what did they do with the surfboard?

Change each singular noun to a plural noun.

4. penny _____   army _____

Day 3

1. What are the four characteristics of mammals?

   _____

   _____

2. To which group of animals does a whale belong? Explain.

   _____

   _____

Day 4

Face north. Look at the compass rose. Name something in your room that is:

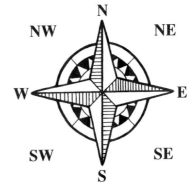

1. northwest of you _____

2. southeast of you _____

3. southwest of you _____

4. northeast of you _____

Name_____

Choose a mammal that interests you. Use the Internet, books, and magazines to learn more about it. Take notes as you find new information. Then, write a report. Use the name of the mammal in the title. Draw a picture of the mammal in its natural habitat. Show the report to your teacher. Make changes if needed.

_____

_____

_____

_____

_____

_____

_____

_____

_____

_____

_____

_____

_____

_____

_____

_____

_____

_____

3.W.2, 3.W.5, 3.W.7, 3.L.1, 3.L.2, 3.OA.A.4, 3.OA.B.5, 3.OA.C.7, 3.NBT.A.2

1. 847 − 358 = _____

2. 6 × _____ = 42   _____ × 9 = 45   9 × 9 = _____

3. 18 ÷ _____ = 2   _____ ÷ 6 = 7   36 ÷ 4 = _____

4. A store's jar of jawbreakers has 50 pieces. Equal amounts of jawbreakers are bought by 5 customers until the jar is empty. How many jawbreakers did each customer buy?

   _____

Redwoods are the tallest trees. In fact, they are the tallest living things in the world. The tallest redwood is taller than a 20-story building. It is so big around that six people holding hands can barely reach around it.

1. What two things are compared in this paragraph? _____

   _____

2. How are the two things alike? _____

   _____

3. How are the two things different? _____

   _____

1. What is **metamorphosis**?

   _____

2. Write numbers **1** through **5** to show the life cycle of the frog.

   _____ Tadpoles hatch and can swim in the water and breathe with gills.

   _____ The tail of the tadpole disappears.

   _____ An egg, covered in a jellylike material, is laid in the water.

   _____ A frog hops out of the water to dry land.

   _____ Lungs and legs grow on the tadpole.

Landforms are any part of Earth's surface. There are rivers, lakes, volcanoes, and mountains. A plain is a flat land with few trees. A cliff is higher than the land below and has steep sides. A peninsula is a piece of land with water on three sides. An island is a tract of land that is surrounded by water on all sides.
Read each sentence. Write **T** if it is true. Write **F** if it is false.

1. _____ A peninsula is surrounded by water on four sides.

2. _____ A plain has very few trees.

3. _____ A cliff has high, steep sides.

4. _____ A volcano is not considered a landform.

Have you ever been to an ocean, a lake, or a mountain? Choose a landform that you have visited. Write about whom you went with and what you did there. Include details to describe thoughts, feelings, and actions. Draw a picture about your writing.

_____

_____

_____

_____

_____

_____

_____

_____

_____

_____

_____

_____

_____

_____

_____

_____

3.RI.3, 3.W.3, 3.OA.A.3, 3.OA.A.4, 3.NBT.A.2

1. _____ × 5 = 45   20 ÷ _____ = 4   _____ ÷ 9 = 8

2. Label $\frac{1}{3}$ on the number line.

3. Label $\frac{2}{3}$ on the number line.

0   1

"A wonderful bird is a pelican; his bill will hold more than his belly can." This is true. A pelican has a big pouch under his bill. The pouch will hold more than 3 gallons (11.36 L) of water, far more than a pelican can hold in his stomach.

1. What is the subject of this passage? _____

2. What word in this paragraph means "a pocket that can hold things"? _____

3. What rhyme is quoted in this paragraph? Underline it.

4. Which is bigger—a pelican's bill or his belly? _____

Draw a line to match each word to its meaning.

1. ecosystem   A. the place an animal lives where all of its needs are met

2. habitat   B. all of the groups of living things living in a place

3. population   C. all of the living and nonliving things in a place

4. environment   D. a group of one kind of living thing living in a place

5. community   E. everything that is around a living thing

6. Name four things that are a part of your classroom environment.

_____

1. Draw a picture of each landform.

volcano   cliff   peninsula

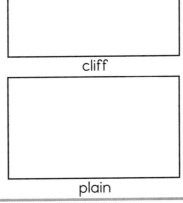

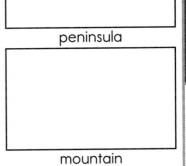

island   plain   mountain

Some days, you think school is a fun place. Other days, you feel like you have already learned everything there is to learn. Or, you feel tired of the same old math class you have been in since the beginning of the school year. Maybe you just need something different! Think of a new subject to study. What would it be? Describe the class as if you are the new teacher. Include details to describe thoughts, feelings, or actions.

_____

_____

_____

_____

_____

_____

_____

_____

_____

_____

_____

_____

_____

_____

_____

_____

_____

_____

_____

_____

_____

_____

3.RI.1, 3.RI.4, 3.RF.3, 3.W.3, 3.L.4, 3.OA.A.4, 3.NF.A.2

Name_____

1. Divide the rectangle into sixths. Label each sixth with the appropriate fraction.

2. In the evening, Lynn helps set up camp. There are 3 rows with 8 tents in each row.
How many tents are there? _____

3. Write **<**, **>**, or **=** to make the statement true.

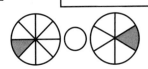

This story continues through Week 25.
Have you ever read stories about sunken treasure buried at the bottom of the ocean? Maybe you have thought how exciting it would be to look for buried gold. But, you may say, people find treasure only in storybooks.

1. What would be a good title for this passage? _____

2. Does the author seem excited or angry? _____

3. What is the main idea of this paragraph? _____

_____

4. Where would you look for buried treasure? _____

_____

1. What is a food chain?

_____

_____

2. Write **1** to **4** to show the order of consumers and producers in a pond food chain.

_____ fish   _____ plant   _____ duck   _____ insect

Write the coordinates for each item.

1. pile of bones _____

2. treasure chest _____

3. spider _____

4. Wonder Cave sign _____

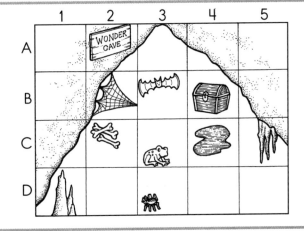

Lost treasure might be found anywhere. That is why some people spend time and money to hunt for buried treasure. Other people find treasure by accident. A couple in California found gold coins worth $10 million when they were walking their dog. What if it was you? What if you found buried treasure? What would you do first? Whom would you tell? What would you do with the money? Include details to describe thoughts, feelings, or actions.

_____

_____

_____

_____

_____

_____

_____

_____

_____

_____

_____

_____

_____

_____

_____

_____

_____

_____

_____

_____

_____

_____

_____

_____

3.RI.1, 3.RI.2, 3.W.3, 3.OA.A.3, 3.NF.A.3, 3.G.A.2

1. Write the fraction for the shape.

    _____

2. Write the missing numbers to complete the pattern.

    3, 6, 12, _____, _____, _____

3. How many inches long is the paper clip? _____

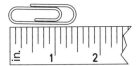

This story began on Week 22.
Kip Wagner from Florida knew treasure was not just in storybooks. He found eight sunken ships loaded with gold and silver. It all started one day in 1948 when Kip was walking along the beach. He saw a blackened lump in the sand and stopped to pick it up. To his surprise, it was a "piece of eight," an old Spanish coin of pure gold.

1. Who is this passage about? _____

2. How many years ago was the "piece of eight" found? _____

3. What is the main idea of this paragraph? _____

4. What did Kip find first? _____

Write **true** or **false**.

1. _____ The rocks on Earth are always changing.

2. _____ Wind and water break old rocks down, which become sedimentary rock.

3. _____ Magma cools and forms metamorphic rocks.

4. _____ Sedimentary rocks can be made into metamorphic rocks.

5. _____ Heat and pressure help form igneous rocks.

George Washington Carver was an inventor who found new ways to use plants. He showed people how to make ink and glue from sweet potatoes. He showed them how to make soap, dye, shampoo, and paper from peanuts. He was also the first person to make peanut butter. George did not patent his ideas. He gave his ideas away for free so that farmers could use them.

1. What did Carver make from sweet potatoes? _____

2. What did Carver make from peanuts? _____

3. What did Carver do with his ideas? _____

If rocks could talk, they would have quite a story to tell. A piece of coal could have formed millions of years ago from trees that grew in a swamp. A rock that sits on a mountaintop might once have been part of the floor of an ocean. Using the Internet, books, and magazines, find out more about how rocks are formed. Then, write a story about what a rock might say if it could talk. Use facts and definitions to explain or inform.

_____

_____

_____

_____

_____

_____

_____

_____

_____

_____

_____

_____

_____

_____

_____

_____

_____

_____

_____

_____

_____

_____

3.RI.1, 3.RI.2, 3.W.2, 3.W.7, 3.W.8, 3.OA.D.9, 3.NF.A.1, 3.MD.B.4

Name_____

1. 396 + 474 = _____

2. 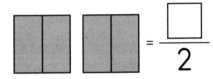 = $\dfrac{\square}{2}$

3. Complete the related multiplication facts.

   20 ÷ 5   5 × ____   18 ÷ 9   9 × ____   36 ÷ 4   4 × ____

Day 1

This story began on Week 22.
Many other people would have taken the coin and gone about their business. But, Kip was interested in where the coin came from and what it was worth. He looked at old maps and read history books until he found information about the coin.

1. Circle words that describe Kip's character.   determined   curious   lazy

2. What was Kip curious about? _____

3. What would you do if you found a gold coin? _____

   _____

4. What is the main idea of this paragraph? _____

Day 2

---

1. Write numbers **1** through **5** to show how a fossil is made.

   _____ The soft parts rot.

   _____ Layers of small rocks, sand, and mud cover the organism.

   _____ The plant or animal dies.

   _____ A print of the organism remains in the rock.

   _____ The pressure of the layers of sediment forms rock.

Day 3

Henry Ford built all kinds of cars. He built the first cars that were low enough in price for many people to buy them. The cars could not go as fast as the cars today. The cars used gas, but the tanks were under the drivers' seats. People had to lift the seats to put gas in the cars. Sometimes, the cars would not start in the cold weather unless people poured hot water under the hoods. Many of the cars did not have bumpers or mirrors because they cost extra money.

1. Compare the cars of today with the cars from the past.

   Similar: _____

   Different: _____

Day 4

Design a new car for the future. Explain what it will do and how it will be powered. What features will it have? How much will it cost? Then, draw your new car and explain your design to a friend.

_____

_____

_____

_____

_____

_____

_____

_____

_____

_____

_____

_____

_____

_____

_____

_____

_____

Name_____

1. Tavaris has 2 pairs of pants hanging in his closet. Each pair of pants has 2 pockets. How many pockets are there in all? _____

2. Write **<**, **>**, or **=** to make the statement true.

3. Complete the related multiplication facts.

   24 ÷ 8   8 × _____   42 ÷ 6   6 × _____   16 ÷ 4   4 × _____

This story began on Week 22.

Kip found out that in the year 1715, a fleet of 11 Spanish ships had been carrying gold, silver, and jewels from South America to Spain. During a storm, the ships sank. "Perhaps," thought Kip, "the ships and their treasure are still at the bottom of the ocean."

1. What is the main idea of this paragraph? _____

2. Which detail about the ships is **not** in this paragraph?

   A. They carried jewels.   B. They sank in a storm.   C. They sank near Florida.

3. What do you think Kip might do? _____

Draw a line to match each landform with its meaning.

1.	mountain	flat land rising above the surrounding land
2.	valley	a wide, flat area of land
3.	canyon	a low place between mountains
4.	plain	a piece of land totally surrounded by water
5.	plateau	a deep valley with steep, high sides
6.	island	a very high, pointed piece of land

China, Italy, and Mexico have given the world different types of foods to enjoy. These are sometimes called ethnic foods. Ways of cooking and eating are part of a group's **culture**. A culture can have a distinctive way of dressing. Other parts of a culture are customs such as festivals or religious ceremonies. A culture can also have its own folktales and myths.

1. Describe your culture. Include how you dress, what foods you eat, and any customs you may have.

   _____

   _____

Imagine that you are given $200 but you are not allowed to keep it. You can only give it away. You have to give it to three different people or charities. How will you divide the money? To whom will you give it? Why? Give reasons to support your opinions. Then, type up your report and show it to a teacher. Make changes if necessary.

_____

_____

_____

_____

_____

_____

_____

_____

_____

_____

_____

_____

_____

_____

_____

_____

_____

_____

_____

_____

_____

_____

_____

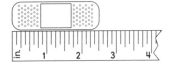

Day 1

1. 603 – 277 = _____

2. How many inches long is the adhesive bandage?

_____

3. Morgan wants to test drive a car and needs the key. Each key ring has 6 keys. If there are 9 key rings, how many keys are there total?

_____

Day 2

Nothing tastes quite as **good** on pancakes or waffles as maple syrup. The native people in eastern Canada made maple syrup a long time ago. Native people from the northern part of the United States made it too.

1. Which word has a **hard g** sound and rhymes with **wood**? _____

2. What other word for **good** could be used in this sentence? _____

3. Circle the sentence in this paragraph that is an opinion.

4. Underline the two sentences in this paragraph that are facts.

Day 3

Circle the best answer.

1. Which is not a property of weather?

   A. land

   B. temperature

   C. wind

   D. precipitation

2. Which of the following affects the weather most?

   A. the clouds

   B. the rain

   C. the sun

   D. the air

Day 4

1. What does the symbol represent? _____

2. What are the three Rs? _____ _____ _____

3. What can you do with clothing you have outgrown? _____

4. How can you recycle, reuse, or reduce at school?

_____

_____

There are many reasons to appreciate trees. They are pretty to look at. They provide shade in the summer. They offer shelter when it rains. Maple syrup comes from trees and makes a breakfast pancake even better. What other gifts come from trees? There are many, and not just for people. Make a list. Use the Internet, books, or magazines to find out more about how trees help us. Then, write a report that combines your own ideas plus other things you learned in your research. Use facts and definitions to explain or inform.

_____

_____

_____

_____

_____

_____

_____

_____

_____

_____

_____

_____

_____

_____

_____

_____

_____

_____

_____

_____

_____

_____

_____

3.RI.4, 3.RF.3, 3.W.2, 3.W.7, 3.W.8, 3.W.10, 3.L.4, 3.OA.A.3, 3.NBT.A.2, 3.MD.B.4   CD-104820 • © Carson-Dellosa

1. Jayla found 11 starfish. Each starfish had 5 arms. How many arms did the starfish have in all? _____

2. Write **<, >,** or **=** to make the statement true.

3. Divide the number line into fourths.

4. Label the fractions $\frac{1}{4}$ and $\frac{3}{4}$.

Day 1

Rewrite the book title with the correct capital letters.

1. *the teeny, tiny woman* _____

Fill in the blank with the correct word.

2. I should _____ finished my homework first (**of, have**).

Place commas, periods, exclamation points, and question marks where they belong.

3. "Did you know that only two types of mammals lay eggs" asked Holly

Fill in the blank with the correct word (**their, they're,** or **there**).

4. "I will carry it over _____ if you will watch the rabbits."

Day 2

Draw a line to match each word to its meaning.

1. water cycle   water when it is a gas

2. evaporation   when heat is removed from a gas, changing it to liquid water

3. condensation   when heat is added to liquid water, changing it to a gas

4. water vapor   the process where water is removed from the surface of Earth and returned back to Earth

Day 3

The exchange of imports and exports is called **trade.** US farmers grow soybeans that countries want to buy. Soybeans are a major US export. The United States does not grow many coffee beans. It imports coffee beans from other countries. Read each description. Circle **import** or **export.**

1. US apples shipped to Russia   import   export

2. TVs from Japan sent to the United States   import   export

3. German cars shipped to the United States   import   export

4. US medical supplies sent to Africa   import   export

Day 4

What are five kinds of water features found on Earth? Use the Internet or books to find out if you do not already know. Write a report that includes a short description of each one. Use facts and definitions to explain and inform. Then, show your report to your teacher. Make changes if needed.

_____

_____

_____

_____

_____

_____

_____

_____

_____

_____

_____

_____

_____

_____

_____

_____

_____

_____

_____

_____

_____

_____

_____

3.W.2, 3.W.4, 3.W.6, 3.W.7, 3.W.8, 3.L.1, 3.L.2, 3.L.3, 3.L.4, 3.OA.A.3, 3.NF.A.2, 3.NF.A.3

1. Round each number to the nearest 10. Then, add.

   212 + 87 is about _____.

2. Are the fractions $\frac{1}{4}$ and $\frac{3}{8}$ equivalent? _____

3. Name two fractions on the number line that are equivalent. _____

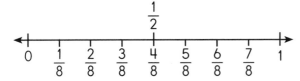

I'm speaking from my home in the Atlantic Ocean off the east coast of the United States. I'm a leatherback turtle, and I'm on the threatened species list along with my friends the green and hawksbill turtles. That scares me! It's tough being a sea turtle!

1. Does the **ough** in **tough** sound like the **ough** in **dough** or in **rough**? _____

2. What is the opposite of **threatened**: safe or endangered? _____

3. What is the turtle's problem? _____

4. Is this a fiction or nonfiction story? _____ How can you tell? _____

   _____

1. Look at the diagram. Label the planets.

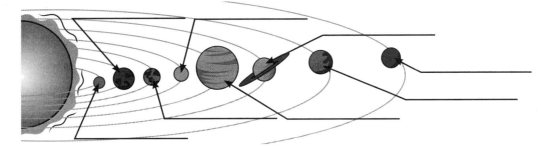

Income is the money a person earns. A person, a family, and a government all receive income. Most people earn income from their jobs. The government gets its income from collecting taxes. Both government and families manage their income with a budget. Their budgets show how they will use the income to pay for things they need and other expenses.

1. How do most people earn their income? _____

2. Name ways you can earn money. _____

   _____

3. How does the government get its income? _____

Name_____

    Imagine that the government has just announced that it will start taxing children's allowances. They will use the taxes to build new parks, schools, and playgrounds. Write a letter to the governor of your state telling him your opinion on taxing children's allowances. Is it a good idea or a bad idea? Is it fair? Share your letter with a friend. Does she share your opinion?

_____

_____

_____

_____

_____

_____

_____

_____

_____

_____

_____

_____

_____

_____

_____

_____

_____

_____

_____

_____

_____

_____

_____

1. Quincey earned 6 stickers a day for 9 days. After 9 days he gave 15 of his stickers to his best friend Tony. How many stickers does Quincey have left?

   _____

2. Use the information below to fill in the line plot.

   Students' Block Towers

   $8\frac{1}{2}$ in. = 5 $9\frac{1}{4}$ in. = 3 $9\frac{1}{2}$ in. = 6

   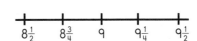

   $8\frac{1}{2}$ $8\frac{3}{4}$ 9 $9\frac{1}{4}$ $9\frac{1}{2}$

Rewrite the book title with the correct capital letters.

1. *there are rocks in my socks* _____

Fill in the blank with the correct word.

2. May I borrow a piece _____ paper? (**of, off**)

Place commas, periods, exclamation points, and question marks where they belong.

3. David asked "What is the longest river"

Fill in the blank with the correct word (**their, they're,** or **there**).

4. Nadia and Liv are feeding _____ pets.

Write a word that correctly completes each sentence.

1. We get day and night because Earth _____ on its axis.

2. It takes _____ hours for Earth to make one rotation.

3. The side of Earth facing away from the sun has _____ .

4. The side of Earth facing toward the sun has _____ .

5. It takes about _____ days for the moon to orbit Earth one time.

Businesses in every industry try to make a profit. To manufacture a product costs money. Businesses must pay their employees and must have a building. To make a profit, the factory owners must sell their products for more money than it costs to make them. The **profit** is the money left over after the expenses are paid.

Read each sentence. Write **T** if it is true. Write **F** if it is false.

1. _____ Most manufacturing takes place in factories.

2. _____ Examples of manufactured products are fire and water.

3. _____ To make a profit, a business must spend more than it earns.

4. _____ An example of an industry is building houses.

Name_____

How old were you four years ago? Think about the things you could not do then that you can do now. How old will you be in four more years? Think about the things you will be able to do then that you cannot do now. Use these facts and your ideas to write an essay about how time brings change to your life. Include details to describe thoughts, feelings, or actions. Then, share your story with two friends. Ask them what they think. Make changes if necessary.

_____

_____

_____

_____

_____

_____

_____

_____

_____

_____

_____

_____

_____

_____

_____

_____

_____

_____

_____

_____

_____

_____

_____

_____

3.W.3, 3.W.5, 3.L.1, 3.L.2, 3.L.3, 3.L.4, 3.OA.D.8, 3.MD.B.4

1. Divide the rectangle into halves and label each half with an appropriate fraction. Then, shade in one-half of the rectangle.

2. Complete the related multiplication facts.

   $32 \div 8$ $8 \times$ ____

   $40 \div 5$ $5 \times$ ____

   $36 \div 6$ $6 \times$ ____

Vasco Núñez de Balboa was born in Spain in 1475. He heard stories about Columbus discovering America. Around 1500, Balboa sailed to Hispaniola, an island near South America. He later traveled to a settlement in Central America called Darien.

1. Whom is this passage about? _____

2. Do you think Balboa grew up speaking English, Spanish, or French? _____

3. How did Balboa travel? _____

4. What effect do you think the stories about Columbus had on Balboa?
   A. They scared him.   B. They made him want to be an explorer.

More than half of all plant and animal species in the world live in the rain forest. Scientists believe that millions more species exist but have not yet been discovered. However, in the last 50 years, nearly half of the rain forests have been destroyed.

1. Why might scientists be concerned about the loss of the rain forests?

   _____

   _____

   _____

   _____

Anyone who buys a product is a **consumer**. A consumer also buys services such as a haircut or a car wash. The businesses that make products or provide services are called **producers**.

1. Name a producer that provides a service.

   _____

2. Explain how a consumer can also be a producer.

   _____

   _____

Imagine that a "new world" has been discovered. The island is far away from any other land. No one has ever been there. No one even knows if there is life on the island. You are one of five people chosen to explore this new world. Write an essay to tell about the experience. Include details to describe thoughts, feelings, or actions.

_____
_____
_____
_____
_____
_____
_____
_____
_____
_____
_____
_____
_____
_____
_____
_____
_____
_____
_____
_____
_____
_____
_____
_____

1. About how much water will a bucket hold?

    A. 5 inches   B. 5 pounds   C. 5 liters   D. 5 ounces

2. 118 + 853 = _____

3. Are these two fractions equivalent? _____

This story continues through Week 34.
It is easy to take sound for granted. But, do you really know what sound is? Sound is caused by something quivering back and forth. This shaking motion is called a **vibration**.

1. What sounds do you hear right now? _____

2. What is a **vibration**? _____

3. Is the second sentence of this paragraph a statement or a question? _____

4. All sound is caused by
    A. music and talking.   B. vibrations in the air.   C. airplanes and machines.

Draw a line to match each word to its meaning.

1. waste   to make something new out of something old

2. reduce   to protect something from destruction

3. reuse   to use less of something

4. recycle   to find a new use for something

5. conserve   something that is thrown out

In an economy based on barter, a farmer might barter or trade vegetables for cloth woven by a traveling weaver. The invention of **currency** meant that the farmer could exchange vegetables for paper money or coins. Then, the farmer could use the money to buy cloth and other products.

1. What is **currency**? _____

2. What does it mean to barter?

    _____

3. What is something you would barter or trade for? _____

    _____

Imagine there is a water shortage in your town. People will have to cut back on the amount of water they use. What can you do to help? Make a list. Use the Internet, books, or magazines to find even more ways to reduce your use of water. Then, write a report that combines your own ideas with what you learned in your research. Use facts and definitions to explain or inform.

_____

_____

_____

_____

_____

_____

_____

_____

_____

_____

_____

_____

_____

_____

_____

_____

_____

_____

_____

_____

_____

_____

3.RI.1, 3.RI.4, 3.W.2, 3.W.7, 3.W.8, 3.W.10, 3.L.4, 3.NBT.A.2, 3.NF.A.3, 3.MD.A.2

CD-104820 • © Carson-Dellosa

Name_____

Day 1

1. 20 × 1 = _____   70 × 4 = _____   80 × 6 = _____

2. What is the area of the rectangle?

   _____ square units

3. A jar of 36 pickles will be divided equally between 4 people. How many pickles will each person get?

   _____

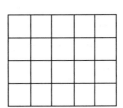

Day 2

This story began on Week 31.
Vibrations travel through the air, and you hear them as sounds. You can hear many sounds at the same time because the air can carry many vibrations at one time.

1. How many syllables does **vibrations** have? _____

2. What is another word or phrase for **many**? _____

3. How many sounds can you hear at the same time?
   A. one   B. more than one

4. The air carries many vibrations, which you hear
   A. as wind.   B. one at a time.   C. as sounds.

Day 3

1. What is a natural resource?

   _____

   _____

2. Write **N** beside each item that is a natural resource.

   _____ air   _____ corn   _____ water

   _____ cow   _____ oil   _____ coal

   _____ shirt   _____ electricity   _____ paper

Day 4

Advertisements are commercials or newspaper ads that try to sell a product to a consumer. People who have jobs in marketing create the ads to make people want to buy their products. Advertisers conduct research to see which group of people would be most likely to buy their products. Advertisers create logos for their products. They may create a special jingle or slogan.

1. Name a place you have seen an advertisement. _____

2. Think of a time you or your family was persuaded to buy something because of an ad. What was it and what made the ad so persuasive? _____

   _____

   _____

Imagine you are the marketing manager of a skateboard company. Your company has just developed an awesome new skateboard. You are in charge of creating the advertising for the new skateboard. Write an ad that includes details to persuade people to choose your skateboard over another company's skateboard. Explain what the new skateboard can do. Use words like **also**, **another**, and **more** to explain its features. Create a slogan or a logo for the new skateboard. Then, draw your advertisement.

_____

_____

_____

_____

_____

_____

_____

_____

_____

_____

_____

_____

_____

1.   Write **<**, **>**, or **=** to make the statement true.

$\frac{5}{8}$ ◯ $\frac{1}{8}$

2.   Draw square units to show the area of the rectangle. Measure the perimeter.

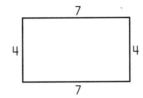

A = _____ sq. units

P = _____ units

This story began on Week 31.
Different sounds are created according to how fast something vibrates. The faster the thing vibrates, the higher the sound. A slower vibration causes a lower sound.

1.   Which two-syllable words in the last sentence rhyme? _____

2.   Write each word's opposite.

faster _____   higher _____

3.   Fill in the blanks. Fast vibrations cause _____ sounds. Slow vibrations cause _____ sounds.

4.   Different sounds are made according to
A. how fast something vibrates.   B. how hot the air is.   C. your hearing.

Bluebirds live in holes they find. The holes may be in trees or in fence posts. People started clearing the land to make roads, buildings, and farms. The bluebird population got smaller. Soon, the bird was added to the endangered list.

1.   Think about what animals need. What did the bluebird not have?

_____

2.   What did people do that caused the bluebird population to get smaller?

_____

Citizens want a government that respects their civil rights. Citizenship brings rights, but it also brings duties. Citizens show civic responsibility in many ways. Civic responsibilities include obeying laws and staying informed about government matters.
Read each sentence. Write **T** if it is true. Write **F** if it is false.

1.   _____ You can show civic responsibility by paying taxes.

2.   _____ Americans are the only people with citizenship.

3.   _____ Civil rights have to do with fairness and justice.

4.   _____ You have to be 18 and over to have civic responsibilities.

Imagine you are a very good artist. Your parents have agreed to let you paint a mural on one of your bedroom walls. What area will your painting be if your painting takes up the entire wall? What will you paint? Describe the scene. Show your essay to your teacher. Make changes if necessary.

_____
_____
_____
_____
_____
_____
_____
_____
_____
_____
_____
_____
_____
_____
_____
_____
_____
_____
_____
_____
_____
_____

3.RI.1, 3.RF.3, 3.W.3, 3.W.4, 3.W.5, 3.L.4, 3.NF.A.3, 3.MD.C.7, 3.MD.D.8

1. 967 – 794 = _____

2. How many children voted in all?

    _____

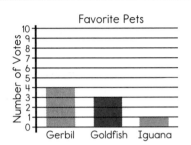

Favorite Pets

3. Brittany parks her car at 3:30. She puts
    enough money in the parking meter for
    60 minutes. What time should she be back at her car? _____

This story began on Week 31.
Unpleasant sounds are called noise. Some noise can be harmful to your hearing. Loud noises, such as those from airplanes and machines, can even cause hearing loss. But, other sounds, such as music or talking, are not dangerous—just pleasant.

1. Which three-syllable word has a prefix that means **not**? _____

2. Which two words in this paragraph are opposites? _____

3. Circle the sounds that might be dangerous to your hearing.
    baby giggling   chainsaw   rock-music concert   kitten meowing

4. Sounds can be _____ or _____ .

Unscramble each word in parentheses to complete the fire safety rule.

1. Put smoke _____ (srcotdeet) near the bedrooms.

2. Make a plan to _____ (speeca) from every room in the house.

3. Choose a place where everyone should meet _____ (duostie).

4. Keep a fire _____ (stuigehrnixe) on each floor in the house.

5. If your _____ (selocht) catch on fire, you should stop, drop, and roll.

The **Liberty** Bell hangs in Philadelphia, Pennsylvania. It was ordered from England in 1751. It was an important symbol for the antislavery movement. It was rung to call meetings and to mark special events. There are many stories of how the bell came to be cracked as it is today. The most common theory is that the large crack happened when the bell was rung to celebrate George Washington's birthday in 1846.

1. What does **liberty** mean? _____

2. Why might the Liberty Bell have been an important symbol for the antislavery
    movement? _____

    _____

    _____

    Sound is all around us. Open a window and you might hear a bird singing or the blare of a car horn. You might hear a rooster crow or a jackhammer blast. A bird song is pretty. The sound of a jackhammer might hurt your ears. What are some sounds that you like? What are some sounds that make your head hurt? Make a list. Then, talk to two or three other students. Ask them how they feel about the sounds you like or dislike. Write an essay about different sounds and how they make people feel.

_____

_____

_____

_____

_____

_____

_____

_____

_____

_____

_____

_____

_____

_____

_____

_____

_____

_____

_____

_____

_____

_____

3.RI.1, 3.RI.2, 3.RF.3, 3.W.3, 3.W.5, 3.W.8, 3.L.4, 3.NBT.A.2, 3.MD.A.1, 3.MD.B.3

1. Jason gets up at 7:00. He takes 15 minutes to shower, 5 minutes to brush his teeth, and 20 minutes to eat breakfast. What time is Jason ready to go to school?

   _____

2. Write **<**, **>**, or **=** to make the statement true.

   $\frac{4}{4}$ ◯ $\frac{1}{4}$

3. 90 × 1 = _____   90 × 6 = _____   80 × 9 = _____

Insects kept eating the leaves of Delia's garden plants. Because pesticides can harm the environment, Delia wanted a natural solution. She found out that most ladybugs eat insect pests but do not damage a garden. Ladybugs make perfect plant guards.

1. Who is the character in this paragraph? _____

2. What is her problem? _____

3. Explain the effect. Pesticides can harm the environment, so _____

   _____.

4. State the cause. Ladybugs make perfect plant guards because _____

   _____.

---

1. What are the five food groups? Give an example of each.

   A. _____

   B. _____

   C. _____

   D. _____

   E. _____

Patriotism is the love and support that a person shows for his country. Patriotism is more noticeable in a national crisis such as an act of terrorism or on national holidays. A patriotic citizen is **loyal** to his country and the values and ideas the country stands for. People can still be patriotic even when they disagree with the government.

1. When is a time you have shown patriotism? _____

2. How did you show it? _____

   _____

3. What does **loyal** mean? _____

Imagine you are the chef at home. What meal will you make for your family for dinner tonight? You may include your favorite foods, but the meal must have something from each of the five food groups. Write an essay about the meal you will make. Describe how you think your family will react to the meal. Give reasons to support your food choices and your opinion.

_____

_____

_____

_____

_____

_____

_____

_____

_____

_____

_____

_____

_____

_____

_____

_____

_____

_____

_____

_____

_____

_____

_____

_____

1.   Round each number to the nearest 100. Then, subtract.

293 – 187 is about _____.

2.   Shade the circle to show the fraction $\frac{6}{6}$.

3.   Circle each shape that has a right angle.

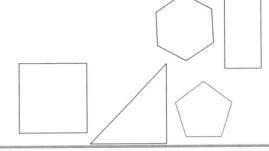

The ancient Mayan Indians lived in Central America and southern Mexico. Today, **descendants** of the Mayan people still live there. During the peak of their civilization, they lived in the tropical rain forests of what is now Guatemala.

1.   Is the **c** in **central** and **civilizations** a **hard c** or a **soft c**? _____

2.   What are **descendants**? _____

3.   What is this passage mostly about?   A. where the Maya live   B. rain forests

4.   Finish this summary sentence. Modern and ancient Mayan people lived in _____
_____.

1.   Name two ways that exercise helps your body.

_____

_____

2.   What might happen if you did not exercise your muscles?

_____

_____

On Memorial Day, Americans remember people in the armed forces who gave their lives for their country. On July 4, Americans celebrate Independence Day. This day reminds Americans of the signing of a document declaring America's independence from Great Britain. Labor Day is a special holiday to celebrate all of the people who work. Read the sentence. Then, write the national holiday it describes.

1.   Americans remember soldiers by placing flags on their graves. _____

2.   Americans celebrate their independence with fireworks. _____

3.   Americans appreciate workers who contribute to the prosperity of the United States.

_____

Think of a time you celebrated Independence Day, Memorial Day, or Labor Day. Whom did you celebrate with? What did you do? Did you eat any special foods? Did you travel anywhere special to celebrate? Include details to describe thoughts, feelings, or actions.

_____

_____

_____

_____

_____

_____

_____

_____

_____

_____

_____

_____

_____

_____

_____

_____

_____

_____

_____

_____

_____

_____

_____

3.RI.2, 3.RI.4, 3.RF.3, 3.W.3, 3.L.4, 3.NBT.A.1, 3.NBT.A.2, 3.NF.A.1, 3.G.A.1

Name_____

Day 1

1. Write a related division sentence for each equation.

    6 × 2 = 12 _____   8 × 7 = 56 _____

2. How many inches long is the feather?

    _____

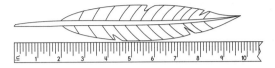

3. Ms. McDonough's class must watch a movie that is 60 minutes long. She wants to divide the movie into 3 equal periods to watch. How many minutes will each movie-watching period be? _____

Day 2

Pete ran into the kitchen to get a drink of water. He spied his jar of marbles sitting open on the kitchen table. Pete slipped on some water spilled on the floor. Pete's arm crashed into the table and upset the marble jar.

1. What is the root word of the word **spied**? _____

2. What other word could you use instead of **spied**? _____

3. What action started the accident? _____

4. Predict what will happen next. _____

Day 3

Moving water has energy. People long ago used water energy to turn large rock wheels to grind corn and wheat into flour. People still use water energy today. They build large dams to hold water in lakes. When the water is released, it turns large turbines. The turbines power generators, which produce electric energy. The electricity moves through power lines to light and heat buildings.

1. Is it possible for all electricity to be powered by water? Why or why not?

    _____

    _____

Day 4

Harriet Tubman was born around 1820 in Maryland. In 1849, she used the Underground Railroad to escape and free herself from slavery. Between 1850 and 1860, she returned to the South several times and helped over 300 slaves escape to freedom. When the Civil War started in 1861, she became a spy for the North. When she was not a spy, she worked as a nurse. In 1857, Harriet bought a home in Auburn, New York. She died in Auburn in 1913.

1. Create a time line of Harriet Tubman's life using the information in the passage.

    _____

Think about the classic story *The Three Little Pigs*. Did you like the ending? Is there a way the wolf could have been nicer? Is there a way the last pig could have made his house wolf-proof? Rewrite the story of *The Three Little Pigs*. Give the story a new ending. Then, share your story with classmates. Type your story on a computer.

_____

_____

_____

_____

_____

_____

_____

_____

_____

_____

_____

_____

_____

_____

_____

_____

_____

_____

_____

_____

_____

_____

_____

_____

1. Write the missing numbers to complete the pattern.

    185, 210, 235, _____, _____, _____

2. Draw square units to find the area of the rectangle. Measure the perimeter.

    A = _____ sq. units

    P = _____ units

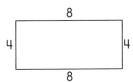

3. 238 + 348 = _____

Rewrite the book title with the correct capital letters.

1. *the book of giant stories* _____

Fill in the blank with the correct word.

2. Gabe borrowed some money _____ his friend. (**off, from**)

Place commas, periods, exclamation points, and question marks where they belong.

3. "According to this book" said Jill "geese fly the highest"

Fill in the blank with the correct word (**their, they're,** or **there**).

4. "Nadia, would you carry this bag of food over _____?" asked Liv.

1. Name four ways that people use computer technology to communicate.

    _____

    _____

    _____

    _____

1. Think of a person or a past event that you think deserves a monument. Draw the monument. Then, describe it with its name, what it symbolizes, what it is made of, and where it would be located.

    _____

    _____

Name_____

A book review is different than a book report. It is one person's reaction to a book. Choose a book you have read in the past. Think about the plot and the characters. Did you connect with any of the characters? Did you like the way the author wrote the book? Was the author trying to convey a message? How did you feel after you read it? Put all of the pieces together and write a book review. Give your opinion of the writing and the story. Give reasons to support your opinions. Then, share your review with another student. If she has read the book, does she have a different opinion? If she has not read the book, does she want to now?

_____
_____
_____
_____
_____
_____
_____
_____
_____
_____
_____
_____
_____
_____
_____
_____
_____
_____
_____
_____
_____
_____
_____

3.W.1, 3.W.8, 3.L.1, 3.L.2, 3.L.3, 3.OA.D.9, 3.NBT.A.2, 3.MD.C.7, 3.MD.D.8

1. Melinda's desk is a trapezoid that has a perimeter of 120 inches, with two diagonal sides that are 24 inches long, and one base that is 39 inches long. How many inches long is the other base? _____

2. Write the missing numbers to complete the pattern.

   500, 475, 450, _____, _____, _____

3. Banks received a small bag of jelly beans as a gift. There are 63 jelly beans in the bag. He wants to share them equally among 7 people. How many will each person get? _____

Warming temperatures caused the glaciers to melt. When the glaciers melted, there were huge holes left where the glaciers used to be. Water from melting glaciers and from rain filled these huge holes. They were no longer holes. They were lakes such as Lake Superior, Lake Michigan, Lake Huron, Lake Erie, and Lake Ontario.

1. Name two lakes that were caused by melting glaciers. _____

2. Where did the water that filled the holes come from? _____

3. Explain the effect. Warming temperatures caused _____.

4. State the cause. Great lakes were formed as a result of _____
   _____.

You probably know the name Beatrix Potter. She wrote and illustrated *The Tale of Peter Rabbit*. However, did you know that Potter was also a botanist, or plant scientist? She studied **fungi**, living things that live on dead plant and animal matter. She collected samples of many different fungi and cut them open to look inside. Then, she painted pictures filled with details to show what they looked like. Amazingly, Potter made over 300 pictures of mushrooms alone.

1. How might Potter's pictures help other scientists?

   _____

   _____

A **decade** is a period of 10 years. A **century** is equal to 100 years. A **millennium** is a period of 1,000 years. The twentieth century lasted from 1901–2000. The first decade of the twenty-first century lasted from 2001-2010.
Circle the word that completes each sentence.

1. Laura's great-grandfather has lived for a (century/decade).

2. The year 2001 was celebrated as the beginning of another (decade/millennium).

3. A 10-year-old child has lived for a (century, decade).

4. We live in the twenty-first (century, decade).

Many women have done important things in the field of science. Marie Curie developed the use of X-rays. Jane Goodall studied wild chimpanzees by sitting and watching them for days. Williamina Fleming never went to school, but in one year alone she discovered 222 stars! Choose one of these women or another female scientist. Use the Internet, books, or magazines to learn more about her. Write a report about her life and her discoveries. Use facts and definitions to explain or inform.

_____

_____

_____

_____

_____

_____

_____

_____

_____

_____

_____

_____

_____

_____

_____

_____

_____

_____

_____

_____

_____

_____

_____

 3.RI.1, 3.RI.3, 3.RI.10, 3.W.2, 3.W.4, 3.W.7, 3.W.8, 3.OA.A.3, 3.OA.D.9, 3.MD.D.8

CD-104820 • © Carson-Dellosa

Day 1

1. Round each number to the nearest 10. Then, subtract.

   578 – 396 is about _____ .

2. A square has one side that measures 6 inches. How many inches is the perimeter of the square? _____

3. Write the fraction. _____

Day 2

Rewrite the sentence with the correct capital letter.

1. sally is a babysitter. _____

Circle the correct verb tense.

2. Carrie (walks, walked) to school yesterday.

Add commas where they are needed.

3. David John and Leo went to the beach.

Write each singular noun as a plural noun.

4. library _____   city _____

Day 3

Thomas Edison had over 1,000 patents with his name on them. A **patent** gives a person or company with an idea the right to be the only one who can use, make, or sell things with that idea. Edison spent many years learning about electricity and sound. One of his most well-known patents was received for the light bulb. It made using lights in a house safe and useful. It was not too expensive, either.

1. Why would a scientist want to patent an idea?

   _____

   _____

   _____

Day 4

Neil Armstrong, Harriet Tubman, and Jane Goodall are famous people who took chances in life. Neil Armstrong took a chance and boarded a spacecraft to the moon. Harriet Tubman took a chance when she helped slaves escape to the North. Jane Goodall took a chance to live in the African wild to study chimpanzees. They all made important contributions to society because they were willing to take chances.

1. What character traits do these famous people have in common?

   _____

2. Is it always a good idea to take a chance on something? _____

   Explain. _____

Think of something you would like to do in life even if you are not sure you could succeed at it. It could be something like playing a new musical instrument or riding a skateboard. After you have picked a challenge, write a plan for how you can succeed at it. Identify each step you will have to take to be successful. Use facts, details, and definitions to explain. Provide a concluding statement.

_____

_____

_____

_____

_____

_____

_____

_____

_____

_____

_____

_____

_____

_____

_____

_____

_____

_____

_____

_____

_____

_____

_____

Answer Key

Page 9
Day 1: 1. 7 sausage pizzas; 2. 300, 600, 300; 3. Check students' answers. 4. 533;
Day 2: 1. blackbirds and a coyote; 2. coyote; 3. fiction; 4. Birds do not gather to sing and dance before they head south for the winter. **Day 3:** 1. ruler, length, centimeters; thermometer, temperature, degrees; balance, mass, grams; beaker, capacity, milliliters; clock, time, seconds; **Day 4:** 1–4. Answers will vary.

Page 10
Answers will vary but should include creative details and an interesting name for a new pizza.

Page 11
Day 1: 1. 56; 2. C; 3. 35 books; **Day 2:** 1. blackbirds; 2. help; Accept any reasonable answer.
3. They liked to have fun. 4. proud; (underlined) I could be the great king of the coyotes.
Day 3: 1. Answers will vary but may include even if scientists cannot understand each other's languages, they can understand all of the measurements made by other scientists around the world. **Day 4:** 1. Answers will vary but may include looking after aging neighbors or cleaning up a park. 2. Answers will vary but may include a library.

Page 12
Answers will vary but should include step-by-step instructions on learning how to ride a two-wheeled bike. The details should include safety tips.

Page 13
Day 1: 1. 289; 2. 500 + 40 + 8; 3. 67, 23;
Day 2: 1. **oo** as in **boot**; 2. the blackbirds' feathers; 3–4. Answers will vary.

Page 13
Day 3: 1. graduated cylinder; 2. mass; 3. volume; 4. balance; **Day 4:** 1. Answers will vary but may include paying to have the window fixed. 2. Answers will vary.

Page 14
Answers will vary but should include facts and show evidence of research.

Page 15
Day 1: 1. 20 flags; 2. ; 3. 289;
Day 2: 1. jabbed; 2. Yes, because he wanted to be king of the coyotes. 3–4. Answers will vary.
Day 3: 1. 3, 2, 4, 5, 1; **Day 4:** 1. Answers will vary. 2. Answers will vary.

Page 16
Answers will vary but should include facts, definitions, and details about the law.

Page 17
Day 1: 1. $\frac{1}{3}$; 2. 170; 3. 146 feet; **Day 2:** 1. "Rudy's Rowdy Robots"; 2. a lilac, an Indian paintbrush; 3. Does Ivan live in Illinois, Idaho, or Iowa? 4. child, tomato; **Day 3:** 1. Answers will vary but may include to draw conclusions, classify data, and display data. **Day 4:** 1. Answers will vary. Allow opportunity for students to share their solutions with classmates.

Page 18
Answers will vary but should show recollection of personal experience. Allow opportunity for students to share their essays with classmates.

Page 19
Day 1: 1. 209; 2. >, <, =; 3. 794, 994; 4. 75, 78, 81; **Day 2:** 1. Southwestern; 2. a Navajo home made of wood and mud; 3. (underlined) Their homes, called hogans, were made of wood and mud and were built in different shapes. 4. Hogans were shaped like domes, or hogans were shaped like hexagons or octagons.
Day 3: 1. experimentation; 2. hypothesis; 3. presentation; 4. conclusion; **Day 4:** 1. an entrance to the United States; 2. people from other countries; 3. the Golden Door

Page 20
Answers will vary but should include feelings, thoughts, and actions. Review students' stories and offer suggestions if needed. Allow time for revision.

Page 21
Day 1: 1. 601; 2. 8 students; 3. circle;
Day 2: 1. Alex, Tuesdays, Thursdays; 2. (circled) drinks; 3. trees' or tree's; 4. (circled) monkeys; **Day 3:** 1. Answers will vary but may include she was watchful, and she communicated information she learned.
Day 4: 1. F; 2. T; 3. T

Page 22
Answers will vary but should offer new information (gained from research) about Jane Goodall's work and an opinion with reasons to support it.

Page 23
Day 1: 1. 20 pictures; 2. 80 or 8 tens; 3. Check students' coloring. **Day 2:** 1. owls; 2. communicate; 3. mew; 4. howls, noises, and movements; **Day 3:** 1. Atoms are the smallest pieces of matter and cannot be seen. 2. gas; 3. solid; 4. liquid; **Day 4:** 1. *Santa Maria*, *Pinta*, *Niña*; 2. to find a new trade route to Asia; 3. Answers will vary but may include that he was trying to find wealth and new lands for his country.

Page 24
Answers will vary but should include facts, definitions, and details to explain how they would convince the queen to fund the trip.

Page 25
Day 1: 1. 440 seats; 2. $2.50; 3. 723; 4. 690; **Day 2:** 1. *The Biography of Helen Keller*; 2. (circled) will, (underlined) teach; 3. your; **Day 3:** 1. friction; 2. lubricant; 3. inertia; 4. speed; **Day 4:** 1. Who: Orville and Wilbur Wright; What: first motor-powered flight; When: December 17, 1903; Where: Kitty Hawk, North Carolina; Why: They loved the idea of flying.

Page 26
Answers will vary but should include an opinion and reasons to support it.

Page 27
Day 1: 1. 9 cars; 2. 751, 485; 3. 339; **Day 2:** 1. Japan; 2. spring; 3. outside, because families eat under the trees; 4. Answers will vary. **Day 3:** 1. lever; 2. inclined plane; 3. wedge; 4. pulley; 5. screw; 6. wheel and axle or pulley; 7. inclined plane or wedge; 8. lever; **Day 4:** 1. executive; legislative; judicial

Answer Key

Page 28
Answers will vary but should describe thoughts, feelings, or actions. Allow time for revision.

Page 29
Day 1: 1. A; 2. 212; 3. 8, 10, 18; **Day 2:** 1. Have; 2. (circled) longest; 3. isn't, is not; shouldn't, should not; 4. women, potatoes; **Day 3:** 1. A rainbow forms when sunlight enters a raindrop. The light bends, or refracts, as it enters the water. Since visible light wavelengths travel at different speeds, they bend at different angles and the colors separate. **Day 4:** 1. 35; 2. four; 3. $400,000 per year

Page 30
Answers will vary but should describe thoughts, feelings, or actions.

Page 31
Day 1: 1. 0, 0, 4; 2. 250; 3. 14 miles; 4. 50, 48, 46; **Day 2:** 1. knight in training; 2. letter; 3. the author's father; 4. interesting; **Day 3:** 1. lightning, electricity, burning candle, cooking food, sun, fireworks; 2. Heat is when thermal energy moves from one place to another. **Day 4:** 1. his inauguration; 2. January 20 every four years; 3. the Founding Fathers of the United States

Page 32
Answers will vary but should include statements that reflect students' opinions on what a president should promise.

Page 33
Day 1: 1. 32 bags; 2. 110; 3. 3 x 3 = 9; **Day 2:** 1. Mrs. Hannah Chadwick, Pine Street, Garnet, Montana; 2. ate; 3. Tony said, "I like dogs to." 4. (strike through) to, too,

Page 34
Answers will vary. Review students' reports and offer suggestions if needed. Allow time for revision.

Page 35
Day 1: 1. 802; 2. sunny; 3. B; **Day 2:** 1. A; 2. winter; 3. on frozen lakes; 4. Fishing in Winter; **Day 3:** 1. compass; 2. north; 3. attract; 4. repel; 5. poles; **Day 4:** 1. Answers will vary but may include cell phones have gotten smaller. 2. Answers will vary but may include that people have easier access to a phone in case of emergencies or that some cell phones let you access the Internet to get information quickly.

Page 36
Answers will vary but should include an opinion and reasons to support it.

Page 37
Day 1: 1. 7, 4, 27; 2. Check students' answers. 3. $16; 4. 16, 9, 18; **Day 2:** 1. homeless; 2. tangled; 3. He is homeless and needs to find food. 4. He found a house where the owners put out a bowl of tuna every morning. **Day 3:** 1. cells; 2. energy; **Day 4:** 1. born in that place or region; 2. played games; 3. dried meat and fish

Page 38
Answers will vary. Check for proper use of quotation marks.

Page 39
Day 1: 1. 4, 15, 7; 2. 9:18; 3. 28, 63, 40;
Day 2: 1. (circled) normally, commonly;
2. Students from another class checked them out. 3. frustrated; 4. Answers will vary.
Day 3: 1. Answers will vary but may include snakes inherit their skin color, which helps camouflage them. 2. Answers will vary but may include polar bears inherit their thick fur, which helps protect them from the cold. 3. Answers will vary but may include camels inherit the ability to go without water for long periods which helps them survive in the desert.
Day 4: 1. *Apollo 11*; 2. Neil Armstrong and Buzz Aldrin; 3. They collected moon rocks and soil samples.

Page 40
Answers will vary but should include thoughts, feelings, and actions.

Page 41
Day 1: 1. 150, 240, 200; 2. 24 gingerbread men; 3. 732; 4. 6, 56, 7; **Day 2:** 1. Lake Superior, United States; 2. F; 3. I want to fly my kite.
Day 3: 1. true; 2. false; Chlorophyll is a green pigment that helps plants absorb sunlight. 3. true; 4. true; 5. false; Plants give off oxygen as waste. **Day 4:** 1. F; 2. T; 3. T

Page 42
Answers will vary but should be based on interview notes. Essays should include an opinion that is supported with reasons.

Page 43
Day 1: 1. 8 pounds; 2. 449; 3. 14, 21, 28, 35;
Day 2: 1. Laura Ingalls Wilder; 2. writing books; 3. hardships; 4. Answers will vary.
Day 3: 1. migrate, goose; 2. adapt, arctic hare; 3. hibernate, bear; **Day 4:** 1. Check students' drawings. 2. Check students' drawings. 3. Check students' coloring. 4. equator

Page 44
Answers will vary but should describe thoughts, feelings, or actions.

Page 45
Day 1: 1. 20 seedlings; 2. 434 miles; 3. Answers will vary. 4. 3, 5, 9; **Day 2:** 1. Aunt Irene, Culver City, California, April; 2. sits; 3. Well, what did they do with the surfboard? 4. pennies, armies; **Day 3:** 1. Answers will vary but may include mammals breathe with lungs. They are warm-blooded. They have fur or hair. Female mammals give birth to live young and feed their young with milk from their bodies.
2. mammals; Answers will vary but may include whales give birth to live offspring, feed their young with milk from their bodies, have backbones, breathe with lungs, and are warm-blooded. **Day 4:** 1–4. Check students' answers.

Page 46
Reports will vary but should be based on research. Allow time for revision.

Page 47
Day 1: 1. 489; 2. 7, 5, 81; 3. 9, 42, 9; 4. 10 jawbreakers; **Day 2:** 1. redwood tree and a 20-story building; 2. Both are tall. 3. Answers may vary but should include trees are living things and buildings are nonliving things. **Day 3:** 1. Metamorphosis is a major developmental change some animals experience as they grow from egg to adult.
2. 2, 4, 1, 5, 3; **Day 4:** 1. F; 2. T; 3. T; 4. F

Page 48
Answers will vary but should include thoughts, feelings, and actions.

Page 49

Day 1: 1. 9, 5, 72; 2–3.

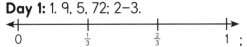

Day 2: 1. pelicans; 2. pouch; 3. (underlined) "A wonderful bird is a pelican; his bill will hold more than his belly can." 4. bill; **Day 3:** 1. C; 2. A; 3. D; 4. E; 5. B; 6. Answers will vary but may include students, teacher, books, desk, rulers, or pencils. **Day 4:** 1. Check students' drawings.

Page 50

Answers will vary but should describe thoughts, feelings, or actions.

Page 51

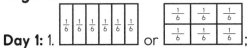

Day 1: 1. [figure] or [figure]; 2. 24 tents; 3. <; **Day 2:** 1. Answers will vary but may include "Sunken Treasure". 2. excited; 3. It is exciting to think about buried treasure, but it does not seem real. 4. Answers will vary. **Day 3:** 1. A food chain shows the flow of energy. 2. 3, 1, 4, 2; **Day 4:** 1. (C,2); 2. (B,4); 3. (D,3); 4. (A,2)

Page 52

Answers will vary but should describe thoughts, feelings, or actions.

Page 53

Day 1: 1. $\frac{3}{4}$; 2. 24, 48, 96; 3. $1\frac{1}{2}$ inches; **Day 2:** 1. Kip Wagner; 2. Answers will vary depending on the current year. 3. A man in Florida found treasure. 4. an old Spanish coin; **Day 3:** 1. true; 2. true; 3. false; 4. true; 5. false; **Day 4:** 1. ink and glue; 2. soap, dye, shampoo, peanut butter, and paper; 3. He shared his ideas with farmers.

Page 54

Answers will vary. Stories should be imaginary but based on real facts.

Page 55

Day 1: 1. 870; 2. 4; 3. 4, 2, 9; **Day 2:** 1. (circled) determined, curious; 2. where the coin came from and what it was worth; 3. Answers will vary. 4. Kip became interested in learning more about the old coin. **Day 3:** 1. 3, 2, 1, 5, 4; **Day 4:** 1. Answers will vary but may include these comparisons. Similar: They both are gas powered, and they both have steering wheels. Different: Many cars did not have bumpers or mirrors, and gas tanks were under the driver's seat.

Page 56

Answers will vary but should include facts, definitions and details to explain the design.

Page 57

Day 1: 1. 4 pockets; 2. <; 3. 3, 7, 4; **Day 2:** 1. Kip learned that a ship carrying gold, silver, and jewels had sunk near the location he found the coin. 2. C; 3. Answers will vary. **Day 3:** 1. a very high, pointed piece of land; 2. a low place between mountains; 3. a deep valley with steep, high sides; 4. a wide, flat area of land; 5. flat land rising above the surrounding land; 6. a piece of land totally surrounded by water; **Day 4:** 1. Answers will vary.

Page 58

Answers will vary but should include an opinion that is supported with reasons. Allow time for revision.

Page 59
Day 1: 1. 326; 2. $2\frac{1}{2}$ inches; 3. 54 keys;
Day 2: 1. good; 2. Answer will vary but may include delicious or yummy. 3. (circled) Nothing tastes quite as good on pancakes or waffles as maple syrup. 4. (underlined) The native people in eastern Canada made maple syrup a long time ago. Native people from the northern part of the United States made it too.
Day 3: 1. A; 2. C; **Day 4:** 1. It is the recycling symbol. 2. reduce, reuse, recycle; 3. Answers will vary but may include giving them to a sibling or friend. 4. Answers will vary but may include throwing water bottles from snack time into the recycling bin.

Page 60
Answers will vary but should include ideas and facts.

Page 61
Day 1: 1. 55 arms; 2. <;
3–4. 0, $\frac{1}{4}$, $\frac{3}{4}$, 1 ;
Day 2: 1. *The Teeny, Tiny Woman*; 2. have; 3. "Did you know that only two types of mammals lay eggs?" asked Holly. 4. there; **Day 3:** 1. the process where water is removed from the surface of Earth and returned back to Earth; 2. when heat is added to liquid water, changing it to a gas; 3. when heat is removed from a gas, changing it to a liquid water; 4. water when it is a gas; **Day 4:** 1. export; 2. import; 3. import; 4. export

Page 62
Answers will vary but may include oceans, rivers, streams, brooks, ponds, lakes, gulfs, or tributaries. Allow time for revision.

Page 63
Day 1: 1. 300; 2. no; 3. $\frac{1}{2}$ and $\frac{4}{8}$; **Day 2:** 1. rough; 2. safe; 3. It belongs to a threatened species. 4. fiction, because turtles do not talk;
Day 3: 1. from the left: Mercury, Venus, Earth, Mars, Jupiter, Saturn, Uranus, Neptune;
Day 4: 1. People earn income from their jobs. 2. Answers will vary but may include doing chores. 3. tax collection

Page 64
Answers will vary but should include reasons to support students' opinions.

Page 65
Day 1: 1. 39 stickers; 2. Check students' line plots.
Day 2: 1. *There Are Rocks in My Socks*; 2. of; 3. David asked, "What is the longest river?" 4. their; **Day 3:** 1. rotates; 2. 24; 3. night; 4. day; 5. 28; **Day 4:** 1. T; 2. F; 3. F; 4. T

Page 66
Answers will vary but should show personal reflection and include details to describe thoughts, feelings, or actions.

Page 67
Day 1: 1. Check students' fractions and shading. 2. 4, 8, 6; **Day 2:** 1. Vasco Núñez de Balboa; 2. Spanish; 3. by ship; 4. B; **Day 3:** 1. Answers will vary but may include scientists might be concerned because animals and plants that we do not even know about are dying. They might be important to the balance of the rain forest.
Day 4: 1. Answers will vary but may include a lawyer or barber. 2. Answers will vary but may include when a person grows their own food, prepares it, and eats it.

Page 68
Answers will vary but should include details to describe thoughts, feelings, or actions.

Page 69
Day 1: 1. C; 2. 971; 3. no; **Day 2:** 1. Answers will vary. 2. a shaking motion; 3. question; 4. B; **Day 3:** 1. something that is thrown out; 2. to use less of something; 3. to find a new use for something; 4. to make something new out of something old; 5. to protect something from destruction; **Day 4:** 1. money; 2. to trade or exchange one thing for another; 3. Answers will vary.

Page 70
Answers will vary but should include facts and definitions to explain or inform.

Page 71
Day 1: 1. 20, 280, 480; 2. 20; 3. 9 pickles; **Day 2:** 1. three; 2. lots, several, numerous; 3. B; 4. C; **Day 3:** 1. A natural resource is something in nature that living things use. 2. air, cow, corn, oil, water, coal; **Day 4:** 1. Answers will vary but may include billboards, magazines, and the Internet. 2. Answers will vary.

Page 72
Answers will vary but should include linking words and phrases.

Page 73
Day 1: 1. >; 2. [grid], 28, 22; **Day 2:** 1. slower and lower; 2. slower; lower; 3. higher, lower; 4. A; **Day 3:** 1. The bluebird did not have the proper shelter. 2. People changed the land and removed the bluebird's habitat. **Day 4:** 1. T; 2. F; 3. T; 4. F

Page 74
Answers will vary but should include details to describe thoughts, feelings, or actions. Allow time for revision.

Page 75
Day 1: 1. 173; 2. 8 children; 3. 4:30; **Day 2:** 1. unpleasant; 2. pleasant and unpleasant; 3. (circled) chainsaw, rock-music concert; 4. Sounds can be unpleasant or pleasant. **Day 3:** 1. detectors; 2. escape; 3. outside; 4. extinguisher; 5. clothes; **Day 4:** 1. Answers will vary but may include freedom. 2. Answers will vary but may include that the slaves wanted freedom.

Page 76
Answers will vary but should describe thoughts or feelings based on personal experience and that of other students.

Page 77
Day 1: 1. 7:40; 2. >; 3. 90, 540, 720; **Day 2:** 1. Delia; 2. Insects were eating her garden plants. 3. Delia wants to find a natural solution. 4. they eat insect pests but do not damage a garden. **Day 3:** 1. grains, vegetables, fruits, dairy, and proteins; Examples will vary. **Day 4:** 1. Answers will vary but may include when students have recited the Pledge of Allegiance. 2. Answers will vary but may include putting their hand over their heart when they took a pledge. 3. Answers will vary but may include to stay true to or support faithfully.

Page 78
Answers will vary but should include appropriate choices from the food groups, an opinion, and reasons to support it.

Page 79
Day 1: 1. 100; 2. ; 3. Check students' answers. **Day 2:** 1. soft c; 2. relatives of people who came before; 3. A; 4. Central America and southern Mexico; **Day 3:** 1. Exercise makes the body strong, helps control weight, helps control stress, improves sleep, and prevents illness. 2. The muscles get smaller and cannot work as well. Weak muscles can be more easily injured when doing activities or moving suddenly. **Day 4:** 1. Memorial Day; 2. Independence Day; 3. Labor Day

Page 80
Answers will vary but should describe thoughts, feelings, or actions.

Page 81
Day 1: 1. 12 ÷ 6 = 2 or 12 ÷ 2 = 6, 56 ÷ 8 = 7 or 56 ÷ 7 = 8; 2. $9\frac{3}{4}$ inches; 3. 20 minutes; **Day 2:** 1. spy; 2. Answers will vary but may include saw, noticed, or spotted. 3. Pete running to the kitchen; 4. Answers will vary. **Day 3:** 1. Not all power can come from water because there are many places on Earth that do not have access to enough water. **Day 4:** 1. Check students' time lines for accuracy.

Page 82
Answers will vary but should have a different ending from the original story.

Page 83
Day 1: 1. 260, 285, 310; 2. , 32, 24; 3. 586; **Day 2:** 1. *The Book of Giant Stories*; 2. from; 3. "According to this book," said Jill, "geese fly the highest." 4. there; **Day 3:** 1. Answers will vary but may include email, blogs, personal websites, cameras, and microphones. **Day 4:** 1. Drawings and answers will vary.

Page 84
Answers will vary but should cover a book the student has read and include an opinion and reasons to support it. Allow time for students to share their reviews.

Page 85
Day 1: 1. 33 inches; 2. 425, 400, 375; 3. 9 jelly beans; **Day 2:** 1. (any two) Lake Superior, Lake Michigan, Lake Huron, Lake Erie, or Lake Ontario; 2. melting glaciers and rain; 3. glaciers to melt; 4. melting glaciers filling the large holes with water; **Day 3:** 1. Potter's pictures had many details. Other scientists could look at the pictures and compare the samples to fungi they were studying to see how they were alike and different. **Day 4:** 1. century; 2. millennium; 3. decade; 4. century

Page 86
Answers will vary but should include facts and definitions.

Page 87
Day 1: 1. 180; 2. 24 inches; 3. $\frac{2}{8}$; **Day 2:** 1. Sally; 2. (circled) walked; 3. David, John, and Leo went to the beach. 4. libraries, cities; **Day 3:** 1. A scientist would be able to protect his idea and use it to make money. **Day 4:** 1. Answers will vary but may include courage and bravery. 2. Answers will vary but may include taking chances is not a good idea if there may be danger involved.

Page 88
Answers will vary but should include facts, details, and definitions to explain and provide a concluding statement.